PRAISE FOR

# HOW TO PRAY

My friend Elmer Towns has written a book to tell us many different
ways to pray, and I love this book because it tells us how to do the most
important thing in our Christian life: pray. Every believer should learn
something from this book, because there are so many different ways to pray.
Read this book not to learn the different techniques to pray, but
to develop a passion to pray—and then pray.

### DR. YONGGI CHO
Pastor, Yoido Full Gospel Church
Seoul, South Korea

Elmer Towns was president of Winnipeg Bible College (now Providence
College and Theological Seminary) when he asked me to be the dean of
students in 1962. The college was a "faith institution," which meant we
basically prayed for money instead of asking for it. I remember hard times
when the money did not come in and we would have to gather the staff
around the desk to ask each person how much money they absolutely
needed. Then we would divide up the rest (if any) of the money that
was remaining. Many times, we did not receive a paycheck.

I know that Elmer spent much time in prayer during these difficult times.
He even instituted a prayer day at the college in which classes were dismissed
so that the entire day could be given over to prayer. Perhaps this is why this
book on the many different ways to pray is especially interesting to me.
I understand the chapters on desperate prayers and praying in Jesus' name.

I eventually became president of Providence College, and now many of our
early dreams have been realized. Providence College has become one of the
largest evangelical theological seminaries in Canada. We have provincial
recognition and are now able to get a scholarship grant per student from
the provincial government. Today, Providence College is one of the solid
evangelical institutions in Canada. And it all goes back to those early
difficult days when we prayed and trusted God to do the miraculous.

### DR. WILLIAM R. EICHHORST
Former President and First Chancellor,
Providence College and Theological Seminary
Otterburne, Manitoba, Canada

Dr. Towns's refreshing appeal, his conversational approach, his unfolding of simple truths, and his exploring of profound mysteries all make *How to Pray* an easy-to-understand, yet challenging read. If I had never learned to talk with God, I would be most grateful for such a helpful prayer-starter—but having prayed for many years, I am nonetheless grateful for the fresh reminders, warm invitations and stirring incentives this enthusiastic prayer coach gives me to talk with my Lord. Ever the teacher, Dr. Towns activates our response by giving focused assignments to apply the lessons personally and to take action practically. The Lord will use this book to help answer the modern disciples' cry, "Teach us to pray!"

## REV. SYLVIA R. EVANS
Founder and Director, Creative Word Ministries
Instructor, Elim Bible Institute
Lima, New York

I've read almost every book written on prayer and I think that Elmer Towns's new book, *How to Pray*, is absolutely the best that's been written in the past 50 years since I've gone into ministry.

When I first entered ministry, I read everything that I could find on the great deeper-life leaders of a hundred years ago. In my opinion, Elmer Towns has achieved what they achieved, and this book ranks right up there with the best books on prayer that have ever been written.

Those older books on prayer took us deep, and when I read Towns's chapter on "Prayers of Crucifixion," I thought I was reading something that came from the church fathers. This book has also taken us to the heights, for he has tapped into the whole experience of worshiping God. And what about breadth? Towns also believes that great answers to prayer can give great breadth to ministry. As a matter of fact, I like this book so much I want every graduate of Liberty University who pastors a church to read this book so they become men of prayer. By the way, there are 10,000 Liberty graduates who are pastoring a church.

## JERRY FALWELL
Senior Pastor, Thomas Road Baptist Church
Founder and Chancellor, Liberty University
Lynchburg, Virginia

Elmer Towns has the gift of clarity. He addresses the mystery of prayer with an entry-level eloquence, generously drawing upon his personal knowledge of the holy Scriptures. This book will be a great help for those who struggle with effective prayer.

## FR. PETER E. GILLQUIST
Director, Missions and Evangelism
Antiochian Orthodox Christian Archdiocese

This book on the ways to pray is an outstanding study for every Christian, but I especially enjoyed the chapter on praying in Jesus' name. Previously, Elmer Towns wrote a devotional book called *365 Ways to Know God* in which the reading for each day focused on a different name of God. Because I know that praying in Jesus' name gets results, I wanted every family in my church to read this devotional, and I wanted all 2000 of my members to read Elmer's book so that they could know God in a deeper and more intimate way. *How to Pray* carries on Elmer's passion for getting people to know God intimately.

## GORDON GODFREY
Senior Pastor, Marcus Pointe Baptist Church
Pensacola, Florida

I met Elmer Towns over 50 years ago when he was a student at Columbia Bible College. We were going on a Christian service assignment in which I was to preach and he was to lead singing. A number of other students were also with us.

When we stopped at a country restaurant for lunch, I noticed that Elmer did not order anything. I didn't realize that Elmer was penniless at the time (he only had money for meals in the college dining room), but I casually said, "You know, the college will pay for this." Elmer told me that he had prayed for God to supply the food for that meal and that if God did not answer, he was willing to go hungry!

I believe that Elmer Towns has had that type of attitude throughout the years. He prays about everything and leaves himself in God's hands. I trust that you will develop that attitude as you read about the many different ways to pray that Elmer has outlined in this book.

## DR. ROBERTSON MCQUILKIN
President Emeritus, Columbia International University
Columbia, South Carolina

Elmer Towns came to Columbia Bible College (now Columbia International University) immediately after his conversion in 1953. In those days, "believing prayer" was a core value of the college—and that is just as true today. The lessons that Elmer learned while at Columbia Bible College are evident in the pages of this manuscript. I praise God that Elmer is still committed to prayer, and I trust that the many different ways to pray that Elmer discusses in this book will transform people's lives—just as they originally transformed the life of Elmer Towns.

## DR. GEORGE W. MURRAY
President, Columbia International University
Columbia, South Carolina

Elmer Towns and I have both faced cancer, and God has answered the prayers of many people to bring healing to us and restore us back to ministry. I endorse all of the ways to pray mentioned in this book; however, I want you to read carefully the chapter on healing. If you know of anyone who is sick, he or she needs to follow the principles in this chapter. If you are called on to pray for someone who is sick, ask God to give him or her a prayer of faith that saves the sick. I believe this chapter will stimulate your faith to trust God for healing miracles.

## WENDELL SMITH
Senior Pastor, The City Church
Kirkland, Washington


Elmer Towns has been a friend of mine for 10 years, and he is the kind of man that even my children love to be around. I liked him from the very first time I met him because he said to me, "Will you pray for me that I will become godlier?" Not many people have asked that of me—much less a world-renowned church growth expert, Dean of Liberty University, and confidante of major ministers in the Body of Christ.

I believe these different ways to pray discussed in this book come out of the heart of a true "God Chaser." As you read each chapter, look behind the methods and techniques of prayer; look to the person of God Himself. Chase after the Lord as you pray, and you will find Him. May this book change your life by giving you a passion for knowing Christ and making Him known.

## TOMMY TENNEY
GodChasers Network
Pineville, Louisiana


Elmer Towns has been a friend of mine for over 35 years. We have laughed together, studied together and, of course, prayed together. I think it is only natural that his analytical mind would come up with so many different ways to pray. I love this book because it demonstrates that in the final analysis, it is not *how* you pray, but *that* you pray. I encourage everyone to read this book and practice the principles of prayer so that God can use this book to make a great impact for the cause of Christ.

## C. PETER WAGNER
Chancellor, Wagner Leadership Institute
Colorado Springs, Colorado

# HOW TO PRAY

## When You Don't Know What to Say

# ELMER L. TOWNS

**Regal**

From Gospel Light
Ventura, California, U.S.A.

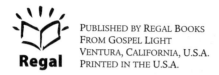

PUBLISHED BY REGAL BOOKS
FROM GOSPEL LIGHT
VENTURA, CALIFORNIA, U.S.A.
PRINTED IN THE U.S.A.

Regal Books is a ministry of Gospel Light, a Christian publisher dedicated to serving the local church. We believe God's vision for Gospel Light is to provide church leaders with biblical, user-friendly materials that will help them evangelize, disciple and minister to children, youth and families.

It is our prayer that this Regal book will help you discover biblical truth for your own life and help you meet the needs of others. May God richly bless you.

For a free catalog of resources from Regal Books/Gospel Light, please call your Christian supplier or contact us at 1-800-4-GOSPEL or www.regalbooks.com.

**Library of Congress Cataloging-in-Publication Data**
Towns, Elmer L.
   How to pray / Elmer L. Towns.
      p. cm.
   ISBN 0-8307-4187-9 (trade paper)
   1. Prayer—Christianity. I. Title.
   BV215.T67 2006
   248.3'2—dc22                                    2006002346


1    2    3    4    5    6    7    8    9    10    /    10    09    08    07    06


Rights for publishing this book in other languages are contracted by Gospel Light World-wide, the international nonprofit ministry of Gospel Light. Gospel Light Worldwide also provides publishing and technical assistance to international publishers dedicated to producing Sunday School and Vacation Bible School curricula and books in the languages of the world. For additional information, visit www.gospellightworldwide.org; write to Gospel Light Worldwide, P.O. Box 3875, Ventura, CA 93006; or send an e-mail to info@gospellightworldwide.org.

# contents

## part 1:
## connecting with god

Following the Model of the Lord's Prayer and
Establishing a Prayer Time with God

## part 2:
# static on the Line

Devotional Readings on How to
Pray in all Circumstances

## part 3:
# A Better Connection

How to Grow and Deepen Our Relationship
with Our Heavenly Father

# introduction

I still remember the thrill I experienced when my son said "da-da" for the first time. There was just something about hearing those simple words that had an impact on me—perhaps because I realized that my son was acknowledging me as his father and attempting to communicate with me. I think that every father feels this way when he hears these simple words from his child.

The same is true of our heavenly Father. When we come to Him in prayer—just talking to Him as a child would talk to his or her father—it thrills our heavenly Father's heart.

Just as there are many ways that a child talks to his or her parent, there are many ways that we can talk to God. For example, when my son became old enough to realize that something he did was wrong, he would say, "Father, I'm sorry." This represents our *prayers of brokenness*—we recognize that we have sinned and ask the Father for forgiveness. When my son had a nightmare, he would cry out, "Daddy, I'm scared!" This represents our *prayers of desperation*—we realize that we need God's comfort and care, and cry out to Him for help. When my son was a little older, he would often say, "Dad, I need five dollars." This type of request represents our *asking prayers*. And of course, then there are all the other little things that children talk about, which reflect our minor (or *minutia*) prayers.

For all these different ways of approaching God in prayer, there are even more ways in which we express our prayers. For instance, in *solo prayer*, we approach God one-on-one with our requests. When we engage in *fellowship prayer*, we join with another person to enjoy time together with God. During *communion prayer*, we soak in God's presence; while in *worship prayer* we glory and magnify the Lord with praise. In addition, during specific times in our lives, we may utter *prayers of faith* when we are absolutely sure that God will answer our request, or we may engage in *warfare prayer* as we fight against temptation, addiction or demonic attack.

Learning to talk to God is as simple as when a baby learns to say "da-da" to his or her father. For those of you who have never prayed, the first chapter of this book, "beginning prayers," will be of great help to you as you seek to delight the Father's heart. The remaining chapters discuss the different ways and methods in which we approach God in prayer. At the end of each chapter is a section called "Your Assignment" that lists some ways in which you can put the material you have just read into practice. It is my hope that through these exercises, you will experience new and refreshing ways to approach God in prayer so that you will desire to connect with God in deeper and more meaningful ways. For when you truly connect with God in prayer, you allow Him to communicate His will for your life.

Elmer Towns
Fall 2005

# Part I:

# Connecting with God

## Following the Model of the Lord's Prayer and Establishing a Prayer Time with God

Prayer is simply a relationship with God. In this section, we will discuss some of the fundamentals of prayer, starting with "beginning prayer," and then follow a model for prayer based on the example that Christ gave to His disciples—the Lord's Prayer. We will cover some of the primary functions of prayer, including establishing intimacy with God, making requests to the Lord, seeking repentance and deliverance, and offering praise and worship to our heavenly Father. This section will then conclude with a few practicalities regarding prayer, such as establishing a time and location for prayer, varying posture in prayer, and praying with others.

# Beginning prayer

*With a God like this loving you, you can pray very simply.*
MATTHEW 6:9, *THE MESSAGE*

I once heard a teenager begin a prayer by saying, "Hi, God!" At first, I thought that while the young man was certainly sincere, his prayer was inappropriate. But as I thought about it, I realized that the question of appropriateness wasn't really mine to ask. Wasn't the real issue, what does *God* think about this young man's prayer? Or for that matter, what does He think about any of our prayers?

## THE RIGHT APPROACH

Some people think that we must be reverent when we pray—closing our eyes, bowing our heads, and using proper language. Others feel that we should approach God more casually, as if we were meeting a friend at Starbucks.

Both approaches deal with what we *say* to God, what we *call* Him, and our *style*—whether we are formal or laid back. The real issue, however, has to do with our *relationship* with God. Didn't Paul say that we should talk to God by calling Him "Father, dear Father" (Rom. 8:15, *NLT*)? To me, that indicates relationship.

How we see our relationship with God affects how we approach Him. In the New Testament, the Greek word most used for "prayer" is *proseuchomai*. This word comes from *pros*, meaning "toward," and *euchomai*, meaning "the face." Thus, prayer means coming to God face-to-face. Watch two people who are in love. They will sit for hours and look deeply into one another's eyes. Look at the way a mother looks into her baby's eyes. Her watchful and caring way expresses her love for that child. That's what prayer is. It's a love relationship.

When we approach God in prayer, we need to realize that He has invited us into His presence. Think about when someone invites us into his or her home. We can tell a lot about how that person feels about us by the way he or she treats us. If the person takes us into the dining room and feeds us, we can assume that he or she has good feelings toward us, or at least wants to impress us. On the other hand, if that individual takes us into the family room to watch TV or into the kitchen to have a snack, we can assume that he or she wants to form a friendship with us. If after eating and watching a video together that person puts us up in the guest room, the bond is even stronger.

When God invites us into His presence, He goes one step farther—He takes us into His very heart. The key to approaching God in prayer is thus finding His heart. Prayer is not about words or about trying to persuade God to do something on our behalf; rather, prayer is about the love relationship with our Creator. One of the Church fathers summarized this idea best when he said that he who prays well, loves well.

## FUZZY IDEAS ABOUT PRAYER

I often hear people say, "I can't pray." They just don't seem to know where to start or what they should say to God. Well, the point is not to focus on what we *can't* do but on what we *can* do. If all we can say is "God," then we can start there. If we can recite

Psalm 23, "The Lord is my shepherd," then we can start there. In fact, we don't even have to say anything. Just coming into God's presence is praying.

Some of us think that we have to get everything in our lives *just right* before we can pray. But that's not the way it is at all. Look at the story of the thief who was dying on the cross next to Jesus. The only thing that he knew about Jesus was that Christ was the Lord. So the thief just said, "Lord, remember me when You come into Your kingdom" (Luke 23:42). It's not the formula of the words we utter that matters, but rather our willingness to open up our heart to God.

Some of us don't pray because we feel that we haven't mastered the mechanics of prayer. It's kind of like those people who refuse to learn how to use a computer because they think it is too complicated. They're afraid to even touch the keyboard. This fear keeps them from communicating with others via e-mail, searching Google, catching up on the news, or doing any of the thousands of other useful things that a computer can help them do. These people's worlds are limited because they won't overcome their mental barriers. The same is true with prayer. We need to put aside our anxiousness and determine to learn how to talk to God.

Some of us worry that we don't have the proper motives when we pray. We fear that we're being selfish . . . or we're feeling distracted . . . or we just don't feel connected to God. Isn't this rather foolish? It's like a man who has fallen into the water but is embarrassed to yell for help. We shouldn't let our worries about having the proper motives keep us from seeking God. We should come to the Father just like a child coming to a parent. Children come to their parents with selfish motives and the most outlandish requests, but they still come. That's the important thing—they come.

# DON'T WAIT!

If we wait to come to God until we have just the right words to say, we may never come. If we wait until we feel that we have the right motives, we may never come. If we wait until we feel that we are "good" enough, we will certainly never come—we are human, so we'll never get everything right. We must just come to the Father as we are.

Think for a moment about a little boy who brings dandelions to his mother. The mother doesn't look at her son's gift and say, "These are weeds!" No, she receives them as though they were roses, because she knows that they were given with love. When the child brings a picture to her that he drew with a big yellow crayon, the mother doesn't say, "What is this scribbling supposed to be?" No, she sees the little child's love for her and accepts it as if it were an artistic masterpiece.

So how do we begin to pray? Very simply: We begin right where we are. We don't have to go to church; we don't have to find a quiet spot; we don't even have to get away from the crowd. We can pray anywhere—even in Times Square on New Year's Eve!

Perhaps we have never prayed before. God says, "Come my children" (Ps. 34:11, *NLT*). Maybe we've been beaten up by sin and don't feel like praying. Jesus says, "Come to Me, all you who labor and are heavy laden, and I will give you rest" (Matt. 11:28). Perhaps we used to pray, but quit. Remember the story of the prodigal son. He said, "I will go home to my Father" (Luke 15:18, *NLT*). Why not do as the prodigal son did? We'll find our Father's arms wide open and ready to receive us.

Just as a child knows what to say when he gets his earthly father's attention, we'll know what to pray after we call God "Father." We need to just open our heart and let it out. God loves us . . . will wait patiently for us to say what's on our heart . . . and will listen to us . So the right way to approach God is just to come!

# YOUR ASSIGNMENT

*Immediately start talking with God.* Before you turn this page or shut this book, pray to your heavenly Father. If you don't know what to say, start by saying, "Lord, I come to You, but I don't know what to say, so help me. Show me how to pray." If you don't feel worthy to come into God's presence, tell that to God as well. Say, "Lord, I don't feel worthy to come into Your presence. Please forgive me of my sins. Thank You."

*Make sure you're a child of God.* Maybe you don't feel like talking to God because you worry that you are not His child. Well, let's run through the following checklist to help you determine your relationship with God:

- ❏ *You realize that God loves you and has a wonderful plan for your life.* Have you realized how much God loves you? That's where you begin. The Bible says, "God so loved the world [including you] that He gave His only begotten Son" (John 3:16).

- ❏ *You realize that your sins have separated you from God.* A sin is simply disobeying what God has told you to do as determined by the Bible. Do you have sin in your life?

- ❏ *You realize the gift of God is Jesus who was punished for your sins.* The story of Jesus' death is well known, but do you realize that Jesus paid for your sins by His death on the cross? "But God showed his great love for us by sending Christ to die for us while we were still sinners" (Rom. 5:8, *NLT*).

❑ *You have accepted God's gift!* When you believe in Jesus Christ, you accept God's gift of forgiveness for your sins—and you receive eternal life (see John 1:12; Rom. 10:9). Have you done this? If not, pray these words now:

> *Dear Lord Jesus, I know that I am a sinner. I believe that You died for my sins and rose from the grave. I now turn from my sins and invite You to come into my heart and life. I receive You as my personal Savior and follow You as my Lord. Amen.*

# CHAPTER TWO

# our model for prayer

*Lord, teach us to pray, as John also taught his disciples.*
LUKE 11:1

As I mentioned, prayer is simply talking face-to-face with God. However, once we begin a routine of talking regularly with God, we will undoubtedly discover that there are many different ways in which to express ourselves to God and many different reasons to pray. The next several chapters discuss some of these different aspects of prayer. But first, let's look at one model of prayer—a prayer known today as the "Lord's Prayer," which was given to us by Jesus while He was on the earth:

*Our Father in heaven,*
*Hallowed be Your name.*
*Your kingdom come.*
*Your will be done*
*On earth as it is in heaven.*
*Give us this day our daily bread.*
*And forgive us our debts,*
*As we forgive our debtors.*
*And do not lead us into temptation,*
*But deliver us from the evil one.*
*For Yours is the kingdom and the power and the glory forever.*
*Amen* (Matt. 6:9-13).

Why examine the Lord's Prayer? Well, suppose that we were told that we only had one minute to talk to the Lord God of heaven. (Obviously, this would never be the case—we can talk to God as long as we want—but play along for a moment.) What would we say to God in that one minute? How would we phrase our words? How would we ensure that we had expressed our needs to God but also communicated our gratitude and thankfulness to Him?

By saying the Lord's Prayer, in one minute we could express everything that we needed to say to God. By saying these simple words, we could be confident that we respectfully acknowledged God, communicated our needs and expressed our gratitude to Him. When we pray the Lord's Prayer, we don't leave anything out—it's the most complete and comprehensive prayer that was ever given to us. Let's take a look at some of the components of the Lord's Prayer to see why this prayer is so effective.

## THE OPENING: ADDRESSING GOD AS OUR FATHER

The Lord's Prayer begins with the phrase, "Our Father." Yes, God is *God*, and surely He is the *Lord*, but Jesus states that we should also recognize Him as our heavenly Father. In other words, Jesus invites us to share in an intimate relationship with God.

Of course, before we can address God as our Father, we first have to be a child of God. I was once walking down the boardwalk in Myrtle Beach, South Carolina, when I felt a tug on my right pocket. Looking down, I saw a little boy pointing to some fluffy pink cotton candy that was whirling around the machine in the vendor's shop.

"I want some," the little boy pleaded.

My first reaction was to buy the little boy a cotton candy cone, because I remember when I was a little boy and didn't even have a nickel for a snack. But because I was not the boy's father, I realized that it really wasn't my place to do this.

"Please . . . please," the boy kept pleading.

"I'm sorry," I said, "I can't—" but before I could finish my sentence, the little boy's father realized what was happening and came over to buy the cotton candy for his son.

The problem was that the little boy wasn't tugging on the pocket of his father. God desires for each of us to recognize Him as our spiritual Father. He wants us to tug on His pocket and ask Him for the needs of our hearts, for He delights in giving us the things for which we ask.

## THE "THY" PETITIONS: PRAYING FOR GOD'S GLORY

After Jesus instructed His disciples to begin their prayers by addressing God as their Father, He next modeled three types of petitions to demonstrate how they should show their reverence and respect for God. These are often called the "Thy" petitions (after the language used in the *King James Version* of the Bible) because they are directed toward God. Let's take a look at these three petitions:

> **Our Father in Heaven . . .**
> 1. "Thy" name be hallowed
> 2. "Thy" kingdom come
> 3. "Thy" will be done
>    . . . on Earth as it is in heaven.

When we pray the first petition, "Hallowed by Thy name," we ask that God's name be revered on the earth—that His name be considered as holy on the earth as it is in heaven. Of course, since God's name is cursed and reviled by many on Earth, this is something that will never be completely answered, because some people will always reject God and refuse to believe in Him. But by stating our desire to see God's name revered, we express our worship to the Lord. Just as the angels sang "holy, holy, holy" to Jesus when He was born, so our hearts should also cry, "Holy is our Father's name!"

The second petition, "Thy kingdom come," is a request for God's guidance and rule in our lives. What does God do in His kingdom? He rules completely. So when we say this portion of the Lord's Prayer, we express our desire to see God's kingdom rule on the earth as completely as His kingdom rules in heaven. In other words, we tell God that each day we will again submit our lives to His rule on Earth, just as He rules in heaven.

When we pray the third petition, "Thy will be done," we surrender (or yield) our lives to the Lord for the present day. Why do we do this? Because God has a plan for our lives *each* day.

During my college days, I worked summers at a camp near Ashville, North Carolina. Late at night, after the other workers had gone to bed, I would be up mopping the floor of the camp's large dining room. One night, I stopped in front of a sign on a post in the middle of the floor that read, "God has a plan for your life." I chuckled to myself and wondered if God's plan for me was to stay up late doing a job for the other guys. I thought of "God's plan" as something far in the distant future—after I had graduated from college. But then it hit me: God had a plan for me *that* day. I was to mop floors. So I bowed my head on the top of the mop handle and yielded that day and that task to God.

"Thy will be done." We must yield every day and everything that we do each day to God.

# THE HINGE: PRAYING FOR OUR PHYSICAL NEEDS

The fourth petition, the "hinge," is the only petition in the Lord's Prayer in which we ask God to provide for our physical needs:

> 4. Give us this day our daily bread.

Of course, when we ask God for our "bread," we mean something more than just the white stuff with the Wonder label on it. "Bread" is a symbolic word that represents all of our daily needs. When we ask for our daily bread, we could be asking God for a job, or for a car to drive to work, or for money to pay our bills, or even for personal healing.

Jesus used the word "bread" because hunger is basic to all of our needs. God gave us an appetite (or hunger) so that we would eat in order to gain strength. If we don't eat food, we can't work, take care of our children, or do any of the other things that we enjoy doing each day. Food is so basic that we can't do anything without "bread." So, when we pray for our daily bread, we ask God to supply the basic elements of life, and we recognize our complete dependence upon Him to supply those needs.

There are two important points to note about this petition. First, when we ask for bread, we are asking for something that is made *here on Earth*. We're not asking for God to perform a miracle by sending manna to us from heaven, nor are we expecting things to come to us as they do in a vending machine—stick in a few quarters and out pops a drink or a pack of peanuts. When we ask for bread, we recognize God's principles for supplying our daily bread—the wheat seed gets planted, harvested and baked into a loaf that we can pick up at the local grocery store. We acknowledge that God is the source of everything and that it is His will for us to have the strength to serve Him each day. Some would have us think that we can demand things from God—

"Name it and claim it!" they say. But God doesn't operate by a vending machine strategy.

Second, when we ask for bread, we are asking God to provide for our needs *each day*. Our bodies have daily needs, so we must pray each day about our particular needs for that day. When we pray, "Give us this day our daily bread," we bring God into our daily struggle for survival. We may be asking Him for a job to earn money so that we can provide for our families, or for wisdom to handle a challenging situation, or just for Him to give us peace of mind. The bottom line is that prayer is about our relationship with God. God wants us to go to Him, tug on His pocket, and ask Him for the needs on our hearts each day. So when God gives us our daily bread, we need to realize that it comes from Him and use it to glorify His name: "Whether you eat or drink, or whatever you do, do all to the glory of God" (1 Cor. 10:31).

This brings up an important question: How much should we ask for when we pray for God to provide our daily bread? If we can pray for bread, can we also pray for some cake or pie . . . or maybe even a few doughnuts? Well, we can certainly pray for necessities, but nowhere in Scripture are we told to pray for luxuries.

In fact, Proverbs 30:8 states, "Remove far from me vanity and lies: give me neither poverty nor riches; feed me with food convenient for me" (*KJV*). What is food that is "convenient" for us? It's like the food we buy at a convenience store. We don't go to a convenience store to buy our whole week's groceries; we just drop in on our way home to get what we need for that day. Asking for daily bread means asking God for enough to get us through that one day.

Why should we pray for bread on a daily basis? "Lest I be full and deny You, and say, 'Who is the LORD?' Or lest I be poor and steal, and profane the name of my God" (Prov. 30:9). If we have too much bread, we forget to rely upon God each day. If we have too little, we may be tempted to break God's commandments and steal. We need enough to satisfy our needs one day at a time.

## THE "US" PETITIONS: PRAYING FOR OUR SPIRITUALITY

The last three petitions in the Lord's Prayer are called the "Us" petitions because they deal with our spiritual lives. Every aspect of Christian living is incorporated in these three final petitions:

> **Give Us This Day Our Daily Bread, and . . .**
> 5. Forgive us our debts
> 6. Do not lead us into temptation
> 7. Deliver us from the evil one

The fifth petition is our request for God's forgiveness: "Forgive us our debts, as we forgive our debtors." Like asking for bread, requesting God's forgiveness is a daily activity—we acknowledge each day that we have fallen short of God's standards and have sinned against Him.

Actually, the issue in this petition is not those sins that could get us "thrown into hell." This is not a prayer for salvation (although some have certainly found Christ when they prayed for forgiveness) but a request to continue our relationship with the Father. All our sins were forgiven when Christ died for us (see John 1:29). In this petition, we ask to be restored to God's fellowship, just as we forgive the debts of others and restore them to our fellowship. So, this petition includes more than just forgiveness; it also teaches us how to live with others.

The sixth petition, "Do not lead us into temptation," deals with our request for God to give us victory over sin—the sin we just asked Him to forgive. Note that we don't ask the Father not to tempt us, because "God cannot be tempted by evil, nor does He Himself tempt anyone" (Jas. 1:13). Also, we don't ask God to quit leading us, because we must have His leadership in our lives. "The LORD is my shepherd . . . He leads me beside the still waters" (Ps. 23:1-2). In this petition, we simply ask God (who always leads us) to keep us from the sin that will overwhelm us. We ask the Father to give us victory.

Finally, the seventh petition is our request for God to protect us from Satan, the evil one. When some people pray the Lord's Prayer, they ask for deliverance from the influence of evil, perhaps because the original *King James Version* of this text only said, "Deliver us from evil." The *New King James Version* identifies the source of evil influence: "the evil one" (Matt. 6:13). (The original Greek word, *poneros*, can be translated as "evil one" or "evil thing.")

## THE BENEDICTION: PRAYING FOR GOD'S KINGDOM TO RULE OUR LIVES

The final benediction, or conclusion, brings it all together and points us to God. When we pray, "Yours is the kingdom," we recognize the rule of God's kingdom in our lives. When we pray, "Yours is the power," we recognize that God has all power to grant our petitions. And when we say, "Yours is the glory forever," we give all the glory and credit to God. *Amen!*

# YOUR ASSIGNMENT

*Memorize the Lord's prayer.* The Lord's prayer given in this chapter is in Matthew 6:9-13; a slightly different version also appears in Luke 11:2-4. This prayer expresses everything you need to pray and everything you need for each day.

*Commit to praying the Lord's Prayer every day.* This chapter has only rippled the surface of this bottomless pool of water called the Lord's Prayer. I began reciting this prayer on a daily basis back in 1982 and was amazed at how many new meanings I discovered in these petitions each day. You can pray this prayer the rest of your life and daily you'll find new strength available to you. I challenge you to pray it every day. For more information on praying the Lord's Prayer, see my book *Praying the Lord's Prayer for Spiritual Breakthrough* (Ventura, CA: Regal Books, 1997).

*Worship the Father using His many names.* See my book *365 Ways to Know God* (Ventura, CA: Regal Books, 2004) or the appendix of *My Father's Names* (Ventura, CA: Regal Books, 1991) for a listing of some of the many names for God (available through Regal Books and at www.elmertowns.com).

*Pray for God's kingdom to come in your life today.* Commit to God each day that you will live your life according to His will.

*Yield yourself to God using the prayer "Your will be done."* God's immediate plan for your life may not be mopping floors at a camp in North Carolina, but He does have something that He wants you to do *each* day. Ask God to fulfill His purpose as you engage in your activities each day.

*Ask God to meet your physical needs today.* Remember, you're not seeking miracles here or asking God to be your personal vending machine—ask God to give you the strength you need to get through just that day. Maybe you could make a prayer list of your needs and give thanks to God when He answers your request. You could then share these answered requests with a friend to help strengthen his or her faith.

*Pray for forgiveness to walk daily in fellowship with the Father.* And don't forget to also forgive anyone who has sinned against you.

*Pray for the Father to keep you from the evil one.* Satan is a roaring lion who seeks to devour you (see 1 Pet. 5:8). For centuries, Christians have prayed the Lord's Prayer and have had their every need met in these seven petitions. So the challenge to you today is to meet your heavenly Father with this prayer. You'll receive the greatest experience on this earth—He'll come to meet you.

CHAPTER 3

# intimacy with God

*Our Father in Heaven, hallowed be Your name.*

MATTHEW 6:9

Now that we have examined the model of prayer that Jesus gave to us, let's take a broader look at some of the components of that prayer. When Jesus taught His disciples how to pray, He began with the words, "Our Father in Heaven" (Matt. 6:9). As mentioned previously, Jesus was inviting His disciples—and *us*—to share in an intimate relationship with God.

It is interesting to note that Jesus was presenting His disciples with an entirely different picture of God than the one to which they were accustomed. In the Old Testament, there does not seem to be as much personal intimacy with God. God was known by the names *Elohim*, the powerful Creator who called the world into existence; *Yahweh (Jehovah)*, the Covenant-keeping deity who told Moses, "I AM that I AM"; and *Adonai*, the One who was the Israelites' master and owner. But not once in the Old Testament was He called "Father" by name or by title. It is true that God was often *likened* unto a father, but this was a metaphor: "But now, O LORD, You are our Father; We are the clay, and You our potter" (Isa. 64:8). For that matter, God was also likened to a mother, but this also was a metaphor: "As one whom his mother comforts, so I will comfort you" (66:13).

But to Jesus, God wasn't just an authoritative father figure. God was His "Papa," a term that indicates His intimate relationship with the Father. Let's examine this relationship in a bit more detail.

## JESUS' VIEW OF GOD AS FATHER

Look for a moment at the story of when Mary and Joseph lost track of the 12-year-old Jesus while they were traveling to Jerusalem (see Luke 2:41-50). When the frantic couple finally found their son in the Temple, Mary exclaimed, "Son, why have You done this to us? Look, Your father and I have sought You anxiously" (v. 48). Jesus seemed a bit surprised at this. "Why did you seek Me?" He said. "Did you not know that I must be about My Father's business?" (v. 49).

When many people read this passage, they put emphasis on the fact that Jesus was found in the house of God, the Temple. Yet they miss the main point of this passage: The first spoken words of Jesus that are recorded in Scripture emphasize His relationship with God. Jesus called God "Father," a name of *intimacy*. Given Mary and Joseph's Old Testament mind-set toward God, it is little wonder that they "did not understand the statement which He spoke to them" (v. 50).

When Jesus was baptized in the Jordan river, the heavenly Father showed up again, saying, "You are My beloved Son; in You I am well pleased" (Luke 3:22). And when Jesus was transfigured before three of His disciples, the Father again reminded the disciples that Jesus had an intimate relationship with Him, saying, "This is My beloved Son. Hear Him!" (Mark 9:7).

This intimacy even plays out during the week before Jesus' death on the cross. Just a few days before He was crucified, Jesus was teaching in the Temple. It was there that He prayed, "Father, save Me from this hour[.] But for this purpose I came to this hour. Father, glorify Your name" (John 12:27-28). The heavenly Father then spoke audibly from Heaven: "I have both glorified it and will glorify it again" (John 12:28).

Some people believe that Jesus' most serious temptation occurred right before He was arrested, when He was praying in the Garden of Gethsemane. "Abba, Father," he prayed, "All things are possible for You. Take this cup away from Me; nevertheless, not what I will, but what You will" (Mark 14:36). Jesus was certainly tempted to bypass the cross, for He knew the horrific physical punishment that lay ahead for Him. But in that moment of crisis, Jesus called on "Abba"—Papa—for help. Based on that prayer and His relationship with the Father, Jesus was strengthened and able to leave the Garden to suffer the punishment of evil men.

Jesus instituted a childlike intimacy between God, the Creator, and us, the created. Paul echoed this idea in his letter to the Galatian church when he told them, "Because you are sons, God has sent forth the Spirit of His Son into your hearts, crying out, 'Abba, Father!'" (Gal. 4:6). The word *"Abba"* that Paul used (our meaning for "Papa") reveals the intimate relationship that we can have with God. Paul also noted that "We are children of God, and if children, then heirs—heirs of God and joint heirs with Christ" (Rom. 8:16-17). We didn't enter the family of God to "receive the spirit of bondage" (v. 15). No! Paul said we all have family rights to cry "Abba, Father."

## ENJOYING THE PRESENCE OF GOD

So where does that leave us? Well, while there are many ways to pray, we ultimately must learn to pray intimately, as a little child talking to his or her father. We may begin with an outward petition, much as any person might when requesting something from a person of authority, but then we can move to the prayer of intimacy. Remember, by its very definition, prayer means to have intimate, face-to-face conversation with God.

What's appealing about the view of our relationship with God that Jesus presented is that it takes all of the pressure off of us to come up with things to say in prayer. Picture little children sitting on the lap of their earthy father. They don't need to say *anything* to their father—just being in the relationship and enjoying their dad's presence is good enough. Our mere presence tells God that we love Him, and His presence reassures us of His love.

But how can we pray without words? When we are in an intimate relationship with the Father, we can simply pray with our feelings. Picture the little children sitting on their father's lap again. They can tell their father that they love him without using any words—their very presence communicates to the father that they love him and want to be with him.

Intimacy in prayer is thus more a matter of being in God's presence than it is about striving to find Him. It is not about methods . . . techniques . . . or even following the right prescription or formula. It is about drawing upon the family relationship we have with the Father through Jesus Christ.

Think about it. The kids on their dad's lap didn't need to take a course to learn how to be his children. It came through birth. Once they were born into his family, they immediately experienced their father's love and began learning how to act as a family member. In the same way, we don't have to learn principles or memorize Scripture to become a child of our heavenly Father. We are His children because He has brought us into His family. As a member of God's family, we can act on our family privilege and enjoy His intimacy now!

# WHEN OUR VIEW OF RELATIONSHIP DOESN'T MATCH

*Wait a minute,* you might be thinking. *All of this intimacy stuff sounds a big too—well, intimate. Doesn't the Bible also tell us that we are to revere God as holy?* Absolutely. In prayer, there is often tension between reverence and relationship. We need to recognize that God is holy and powerful and give Him the reverence that He is due. We need to grab hold of His reverence and plead mercy by the blood of Jesus Christ.

However, we also need to realize that we have a relationship with God. One way that children demonstrate love to their parents is by showing them respect. When children obey their parents' wishes and recognize that they have authority, children show their folks that they value the relationship. When we show reverence to God and "hallow His name," we indicate that we value our relationship with God. We can walk deeply into intimacy with God and know that He loves us, sent His Son to die for us, and has a wonderful plan for our lives.

But what if we don't feel this connection? How do we get past the "request" phase of our relationship with God and feel this intimate connection? Well, the simple answer is to just give it time. Let the relationship develop. After all, babies don't immediately love their fathers or mothers the day they are born. If anything, they are born with their fists clenched.

Babies *are* selfish, technically speaking, and are only concerned with what they can get from their parents. They selfishly mandate that their parents cater to their every whim. They cry when their diapers are wet, when the room is too hot, or when they feel ignored. In a crowded, hushed church service, babies don't consider whether their bawling is interrupting the pastor's message from God. They're not concerned about distracting people from the worship service or even if they are disrupting something that God is saying to a person. No, they are utterly selfish.

But not irreversibly selfish. As time passes and children grow, they learn better ways to express their needs. And typically, in a family relationship, children learn to give love in the same way that they receive it. How do kids learn to love their parents? By being loved! "We love Him because He first loved us" (1 John 4:19).

But what if our earthly fathers are poor models of this type of loving relationship? How can we relate to a picture of a loving heavenly Father when we have no earthly model on which to base this concept? It is important to note that while the illustration of earthly children and fathers makes for some good examples, we shouldn't begin with this concept and then project that relationship onto God. In fact, the opposite is true. We receive our understanding of our earthly fathers *from the divine model.* God is our Papa, but He is also our boss who leads His family. He is our Provider. He is the mighty Creator who protects His family. All of these analogies are true, and they all begin with Him.

Our earthly fathers should not be the model for our relationship with God—our relationship with God should be the model for how we have relationships here on Earth. No matter what the relationship with our earthly fathers looks like, we can't use this as a basis for rejecting a relationship with our divine family. Our past human experiences may make prayers of intimacy difficult for us—especially if abuse occurred in our earthly families—but it shouldn't be impossible. God can heal any past hurt and restore our brokenness. If we forgive our families as God has forgiven us, then that act of forgiveness will lead us down the path to God's victory over any wrong perception.

# YOUR ASSIGNMENT

*Forgive.* If you've had a negative relationship with your earthly father, it's your responsibility to forgive him and get yourself ready for a wonderful relationship with your heavenly Father. You don't forgive your earthly father for his sake; you do it for your sake. You'll never be whole until you do.

*Confess all sins that break your fellowship with the Father.* Study 1 John 1:7-10. Confess any sins that you have in your life and accept God's forgiveness.

*Rest in the Father's presence.* Don't pray outwardly or with words. Just enjoy His presence. Remain in the Father's presence, meditating on His goodness and love.

# asking and receiving

*Your kingdom come. Your will be done on earth as it is*
*in heaven. Give us this day our daily bread.*
MATTHEW 6:10-11

The Lord's Prayer contains seven petitions, or requests, to God. Perhaps this is because Jesus recognized that asking and receiving from God is a big component of prayer. In fact, in John 16:24, Jesus told His disciples, "Until now you have asked nothing in My name. Ask, and you will receive, that your joy may be full."

However, there are many people who think that the idea of asking for things from God is somehow degrading to Him. They believe that asking is like begging or manipulating God. But it is important to remember that the idea of asking began with God, not with us. Very early in Jesus' ministry, He said, "Ask, and it will be given to you; seek, and you will find; knock, and it will be opened to you. For everyone who asks receives, and he who seeks finds, and to him who knocks it will be opened" (Matt. 7:7-8).

This brings up an interesting question: Why does God want His children to ask Him for things? If He is an *all-knowing* God, wouldn't He already *know* our needs before we even ask? And doesn't the Bible teach, "Your Father knows the things you have need of before you ask Him" (Matt. 6:8)? So what's the point? Actually, there are several good reasons why God wants us to ask for things in prayer.

# WHY DOES GOD WANT US TO ASK FOR OUR NEEDS?

Perhaps the primary reason has a lot to do with *trust*. Imagine for a moment that you are planning a birthday party for your sister. You are very busy and have a lot of details to handle—so many, in fact, that you realize that you won't be able to get everything done in time. So you decide to ask one of your friends to help you. Two friends are available: John, who is a bit of a slacker and not terribly good with responsibility; and Bill, who is very reliable and incredibly organized. Which friend do you ask? Well, this should be a no-brainer—you ask Bill, because you trust in his abilities to get the job done.

In the same way, when we ask for something in prayer, we demonstrate our trust in God. When Jesus told His disciples that He would do whatever they asked in His name, He was introducing them to one of the most elementary forms of dependence upon God. When we have to ask something of God, it means that we are dependent upon Him for the answers we need. It's another way of saying that we *trust* Him.

A second reason that we should ask is because God *likes* to be asked. If you are a mother or a father, don't you enjoy it when your children ask you for things? Sure, you probably already know what your kids need, but it is still a good feeling to know they depend on you to provide for them. Parents who love their children *want* them to love them back. Asking for something is the most elementary form of dependence, and love grows in an atmosphere of asking and receiving.

Asking God for things in prayer also puts us into a partnership with our heavenly Father. If we share an office with someone, we have to work with one another, share tasks, and rely on each other for support. We have to ask for what we need and then receive those things from the other person. In the same way, we are coworkers with God in bringing His kingdom to the earth. "For we are God's fellow workers; you are God's field, you are God's building" (1 Cor. 3:9). We partner with God in His great tasks. This partnership is based on a spirit of cooperation and trust.

Of course, this also means that asking for things enriches our fellowship with God. When we tell God what's on our heart and ask for His help, our relationship with our heavenly Father is deepened. We learn to rely on God for strength, and when He answers our prayers, it bolters our faith in Him. God is pleased when we share things of great importance.

But when we say, "I'll not bother God with these minor details," doesn't that imply that we are questioning our relationship with Him? Would we worry about asking a close friend for something that was of importance to us, even if we considered it something minor? Of course not—if we are truly close friends, we would know that the other person would want to help us, no matter how "small" or "insignificant" the request. We can't hide anything from God, anyway, so why try? It just ruins our relationship with Him.

What if we just kept our prayers on the lofty heights of praise, adoration and worship all the time? What if we never shared our problems with God? What if we felt as if we could never ask anything from Him? Would we be acting honestly toward Him? And if we're not being honest with Him regarding our needs, could we honestly be worshiping Him? When we pray and ask God for His help, isn't that evidence of a healthy relationship?

Asking is a rule of the Kingdom. It's the way that small children relate to their parents, and it's the way that God's children should relate to Him. Asking is not a lower form of prayer, nor is it an unsophisticated form of praying. Like breathing air, asking is necessary in order to continue our spiritual walk with God.

## PRAYING IN JESUS' NAME

Jesus said, "Until now you have asked nothing in *My name*" (John 16:24, emphasis added). In John 14:13, Jesus told His disciples, "Whatever you ask in *My name*, that I will do" (emphasis added).

So, was Jesus instructing us to use some sort of mantra? Was He saying that we can just close our prayers with "in Jesus' name, Amen" and be guaranteed that our prayers will be answered? No! This means nothing of the sort. Using Jesus' name in prayer is not a magical key to unlocking heaven's door.

Again, it's all about the relationship. When we pray in Jesus' name, we enter into a relationship with Jesus Christ. We take full advantage of the death of Jesus on the cross as payment for our sins. We accept Him as the Lord over our life and identify ourselves with Christ. We restore our relationship because any sin that has prohibited our access to God has been forgiven. "Behold! The Lamb of God who takes away the sin of the world!" (John 1:29).

Praying in Jesus' name not only identifies us with Jesus' death on the cross, but it also identifies us with the new life of His resurrection. In Ephesians 2:4-6, Paul states:

> But God, who is rich in mercy, because of His great love with which He loved us, even when we were dead in trespasses, made us alive together with Christ . . . and raised us up together, and made us sit together in the heavenly places in Christ Jesus.

So, when we pray in Jesus' name, we can get as close to God the Father as Jesus can. We can't get any closer than that!

The secret of our Christian life is also the secret of praying in Jesus' name. We become Christians by asking Jesus into our lives (see John 1:12; Col. 1:28). The essence of our Christian life is Christ in us and us in Him. Jesus said, "If you abide in Me, and My words abide in you, you will ask what you desire, and it shall be done for you" (John 15:7). Notice the condition here for getting our prayers answered: We must *abide* in Him. So when we pray in Jesus' name, it should remind us of our relationship with the Father and that we are to "get into" Jesus—to abide with Him. This becomes the basis for all answers to prayer.

We can pray in Jesus' name because of the *friendship factor* that we have with Christ. Jesus considers each of us to be His close friends. When we pray in His name, we approach the right hand of the Father and abide with Christ. In other words, we get close to God. And that's the place where our prayers are heard and answered.

# YOUR ASSIGNMENT

*Write a short list of your most urgent requests.* Use the following table to create a list of your most urgent prayer requests. This list could contain two or three items or it could contain a dozen.

| Prayer Request | Date | Answer | Date |
|---|---|---|---|
| 1. | | | |
| 2. | | | |
| 3. | | | |
| 4. | | | |
| 5. | | | |

*Present these requests to God daily.* Keep your list near the place where you usually pray each day, and then ask God for answers to these requests each day. You might want to write a simple explanation of what you want God to do or how you want God to answer.

*Begin your prayers in Jesus' name.* Don't just wait until the end of your prayer to say, "in Jesus' name." Remember that when you pray in Jesus' name, you are entering into a relationship with Jesus Christ. Approach your heavenly Father and abide in Him in prayer. And don't forget to thank Jesus for making this relationship possible!

*Indicate when God answers a request.* I typically write "Amen" next to the prayers that God has answered in my life. When it's a *great* answer, I write it in big letters: AMEN!!

*File away these answers to prayers to encourage your faith later.* I have prayer request lists that stretch back to 1950! Sometimes when I'm feeling discouraged, I look over these past lists and am reminded of all the times that God has answered my prayers. I'm encouraged to go forward and continue to ask God for answers in my present need.

*Begin now!* Don't wait until you've finished this book or until you've developed a habit of praying regularly. If you wait, you might never do it. So start now!

# Repentance and Deliverance

*And forgive us our debts, as we forgive our debtors. And do not
lead us into temptation, but deliver us from the evil one.*

MATTHEW 6:12-13

When we ask God to "forgive us our debts, as we forgive our
debtors," we ask God to continue our relationship with Him. We
ask to be restored to God's fellowship, just as we forgive the
debts of others and restore them to our fellowship. Repentance
implies that we understand that we have broken God's commands and are sorry for what we have done. We acknowledge
that our sins have separated us from having an intimate relationship with the Father.

Many people weep when they first come to Jesus Christ.
They are broken because of their sins and weep over what they
have done. The Gospel of Luke tells the story of one woman who
was so broken over her sin that she stood behind Jesus at His feet
and wept (see Luke 7:38). In Acts 2, when Peter told the unbelieving Jews that they had murdered the Son of God, the people
in the crowd "were cut to the heart, and said to Peter and the rest
of the apostles, 'Men and brethren, what shall we do?'" (v. 37).

## WEEPING IN PRAYER

There's nothing wrong with weeping our way to the cross of Jesus
Christ. However, not all people weep when they get saved. Some

people laugh, because the burden of their sin has been rolled away and they feel an incredible sense of freedom from their past. Some people bow humbly before God. This is what the tax collector did in the story told in Luke: "And the tax collector, standing afar off, would not so much as raise his eyes to heaven, but beat his breast, saying, 'God, be merciful to me a sinner!'" (Luke 18:13).

When I was saved, I didn't cry. I was in a serious mood. I knew that I was lost, so I just prayed, *Lord, I have never done this before.* But in that moment of realization, God enabled me to experience the horrors of hell for a few short seconds. It felt as if I were actually in hell! Quickly, I cried out, "Jesus, come into my heart and save me!" In an instant, He did. I immediately knew that Christ had come into my life. This was an incredibly moving experience in my life, and not once since that time have I ever doubted that I was saved. It was as if I were a man drowning in the ocean and someone had pulled me from the waves and put me on the firm deck of a ship.

However, the fact remains that weeping is part of prayer—especially when we are feeling broken because we know that we need forgiveness or when we are discouraged because of some sin that keeps creeping back into our lives. Why are tears important when we pray?

Perhaps one reason is that tears show the sincerity of our heart. They show the depth of our emotions and indicate that we have reached the very bottom of our heart. Sometimes we hide the pain in our lives by masking it with humor and laughter. Sometimes we use words to mislead and avoid dealing with our hurt. But when we genuinely cry, there's no covering up our emotions. All our deceptions fade away.

## BIBLICAL WEEPERS

Scripture provides us with some great examples of weepers—people who wept before the Lord on all sorts of occasions and for many different reasons. When Mary lost her brother, Lazarus, she wept over the loss of her brother and her disappointment that Jesus had not been there to save him. "Lord, if You had been here," she said to Jesus, "my brother would not have died" (John 11:32). Jesus was so grieved when he heard the news the he also wept over the loss of his friend. If our hearts are breaking, we shouldn't be ashamed to just let the river of tears flow.

When the Israelites were taken captive in the land of Babylon, they wept over the good things that they used to have. "By the rivers of Babylon, there we sat down, yea, we wept when we remembered Zion" (Ps. 137:1). When their captors asked the Jews to sing a happy song, the Israelites responded, "How shall we sing the LORD's song in a foreign land?" (Ps. 137:4). There's a time when we put aside our laughter and weep over the memory of what we have lost. "To everything there is a season . . . A time to weep, and a time to laugh; a time to mourn, and a time to dance" (Eccles. 3:1,4).

And let's not forget Jeremiah, the "weeping prophet." Jeremiah was faithful to the call of God, but he had a rough time of it. When he was punished for his faithfulness by being flogged in the sight of the city, thrown into a dungeon and ridiculed, Jeremiah cried out, "Oh, that my head were waters, and my eyes a fountain of tears, that I might weep day and night for the slain of the daughter of my people!" (Jer. 9:1).

And Paul surely had a prayer of brokenness for his unsaved Jewish brethren. "I have great sorrow and continual grief in my heart. For I could wish that I myself were accursed from Christ for my brethren, my countrymen according to the flesh" (Rom. 9:2-3). Paul felt great pain that his Jewish brothers had rejected Christ as their Lord and Savior. His tears were not for what he had lost, but for others who were lost.

To be an effective intercessor, we must have a "weeping heart" before God. If our eyes are always dry, it means that our soul is also probably dry. And a dry heart eventually becomes a hardened heart. How can we soften our heart before God? Through tears and brokenness.

When we cry before God, it's a sign that God has touched the very center of our being. He has reached into the bottom layer of our heart to scratch away the scab that we dare not touch ourselves. Our tears demonstrate to God our honesty and sincerity in dealing with the core issues. Sometimes it takes brokenness and tears to unseat the pride in our lives and allow our hearts to be exposed.

## REMEMBRANCE OF PAST SINS

Oftentimes it's good when God reminds us of our past sins. The more that we remember our sin, the more the memory of that sin scares us and forces us to go even deeper into repentance. Such was the case with King David after he committed adultery with Bathsheba and, to cover up his guilt, had her husband killed. After Nathan the prophet called him out on his sin, David was so brokenhearted that he cried out to God, "Against You, You only, have I sinned, and done this evil in Your sight" (Ps. 51:4). David couldn't get the memory of this sin out of his head: "For I acknowledge my transgressions," he said, "and my sin is always before me" (v. 3).

Sometimes we know that there is sin in our life, but we just cannot make ourselves repent. Sometimes we know what to do, but we cannot discipline ourselves to do it. It is then that God sends us the conviction of sin. It is then that God breaks our heart so that we weep over our sins. When this happens, tears are good, because tears make us deal with our sin and ask God for His forgiveness.

Peter Cartwright, the Methodist circuit-riding evangelist, prayed for two weeks seeking salvation. He wept continually before God, but he could not shake the feeling that he was going to hell. Finally, Cartwright's mother intervened and prayed for him, assuring him that God loved him and had answered his prayers. Cartwright accepted Christ as his Savior and went on to become a fruitful Methodist preacher, establishing hundreds of churches during his lifetime.[1]

Any time we see someone with tears, we should realize that they are in transition. Of course, we can't spend all of our lives crying—at some point we need to pull ourselves up and move on. But anyone who has prevailed with God has probably cried the way to a new day and a better tomorrow. For inevitably, tears lead to joy and victory.

## DELIVERANCE FROM OUR PAST

While God will sometimes remind us of our past sins in order to get our attention and call us to repentance, it is important to remember that He doesn't want us to remain bound to those past mistakes. Addiction is one way that Satan keeps us in bondage and prevents us from experiencing the true freedom that we all have in Christ. By keeping us tied to our past debilitative habits, Satan attempts to destroy the relationship that God the Father wishes to have with each of us. This is why the writer of Hebrews exhorts us to "lay aside every weight, and the sin which doth so easily beset us, and let us run with patience the race that is set before us" (Heb. 12:1, *KJV*).

"Besetting sins" are those compulsive behaviors that we just can't seem to control. It could be an addiction to cigarettes, alcohol, drugs, sex, or even sports or the entertainment offered by the world. Once we get involved with such practices, debilitating habits form that are extremely difficult to stop.

Addiction begins first in our mind and then gets into our emotions. We first *think* that it would nice to engage in some behavior; later we begin to *feel* that we simply must do it. As the practice is repeated over time, our compulsions settle into physical addiction, and we are hooked! Our physical body cries out for more and suffers withdrawal symptoms when deprived of the debilitating behavior. Paul described this pattern in his letter to the Christians in Rome: "When I want to do good, I don't. And when I try not to do wrong, I do it anyway" (Rom. 7:19, *NLT*).

The final petition in the Lord's Prayer is a request for God to deliver us from Satan, the evil one. Never forget that compulsions are fanned by the devil. Satan is "the father of lies" (John 8:44, *NLT*) and he wants each of us to believe his lies. He is behind every besetting sin that we encounter and uses these sins to manipulate us as his pawns in the chess game of life. When we become willingly obedient to Satan, he wins the battle.

## PRESCRIPTION FOR DELIVERANCE[2]

So how do we break the bonds of addiction? The primary weapon that we have against besetting sins is a heart cleansed by Jesus Christ and a mind filled with His presence. It's all about the battle for our mind. Paul told the Corinthians, "For the weapons of our warfare are not carnal but mighty in God for pulling down strongholds, casting down arguments and every high thing that exalts itself against the knowledge of God, bringing every thought into captivity to the obedience of Christ" (2 Cor. 10:4-5).

### 1. Recognizing Sin in Our Life

The first step to breaking addiction is to recognize any outward control over your mind or your life. This could be any ungodly influence from our past or that is currently in our life, such as the influence of a religious cult, New Age way of thinking, false religions, or anything else that detracts from the truth of God. We should not go easy on ourselves. Jesus said, "Whoever commits sin is a slave of sin" (John 8:34). If we want to be delivered from addiction, we have to be thorough.

The next step is to recognize any self-deception that plunged us into the addiction. Many people who are in bondage refuse to take responsibility for their sins. They blame their behaviors on their families, job pressures, life crises, or anything else that is convenient. But until we take responsibility for *all* of our actions, we cannot break the bondage and experience true deliverance from our sins.

## 2. Filling Our Minds with Christ

Once we've identified any outward influences, the next step to breaking addiction is to fill our mind with Jesus Christ. Jesus is the truth, and therefore knowing Him is a major step toward freedom over addiction. "You shall know the truth, and the truth shall make you free" (John 8:32). A good way to know Christ is by reading and understanding the Scriptures, for God's Word is also truth (see John 17:17).

Freedom from addiction begins with our desires, not with knowing the causes of our bondage or knowing all the gory details. We must make a life-freeing *choice* to be delivered. Because an external power controls our mind and is responsible for our bondage, our deliverance must come from an external power—the power of God. So we must fight the battle over our mind by asking God to help deliver us from the evil one, and then strengthen our mind with the Word of God and the truth of Jesus Christ.

## 3. Fasting and Praying for Deliverance

We must *pray and fast for deliverance* over our besetting sin. In the Gospel of Matthew, the father of a demon-possessed boy brought his son to the disciples for healing. However, the disciples could not cast out the demon and cure the boy. When they asked Jesus about the cause of their failure, the Lord said, "This kind does not go out except by prayer and fasting" (Matt 17:21).

One point that is interesting about the Greek verb tense for "fasting" used in this verse (*nesteia*) is that it suggests continuous action. This indicates that fasting will probably be required more than once to break an addiction. In addition, like all forms of deliverance, the greater the addiction, the more often we will have to fast and pray. The greater the addiction, the more deeply we will need to repent of sin and the closer we will need to get to God.

## 4. Forgiving Others

The next step to freedom is to forgive others who have sinned against us: "Forgive us our debts as we forgive our debtors." A person in bondage is one who complains that a business partner stole his company, or that his family mistreated him, or that his ex-wife was the cause of the divorce and the breakdown of his family. But the person who blames others is merely justifying his own addictive behaviors. Those who continually bring up the past are in bondage to the past. To cut any bondage to our sin, we must be willing to forgive others who may have wronged us. When we refuse to let them off the hook, they keep us on the hook.

Perhaps we don't want to forgive because we fear the consequences. We realize that when we forgive the other person, we give up the right to seek justice against that individual for the betrayal and the pain that he or she caused. The problem is that we probably will never receive the compensation that we believe the other person *owes* us. The executive who chooses to forgive his business partner will have to endure the pain of betrayal and accept the loss of his business. The family member who reconciles with his family will have to swallow his pride and accept the fact that justice was not served. The man who chooses to look at his own actions as the cause of the breakdown of his marriage will have to endure the pain of regret and the loss of time with his children in the subsequent custody arrangement.

Regardless of whether we choose to forgive, we will have to live with the consequences of what has occurred. So shouldn't we just let go of the bitterness and move on? Why should we remain in bondage to people who have wronged us? If we don't forgive them for *their* sake, we should at least get smart and forgive them for *our* sake. We need to choose to forgive and break the power of bondage and sin in our life. We won't have spiritual freedom until we forgive the sins of others, as God has forgiven our sins.

## PUTTING OUR DELIVERANCE IN GOD'S HANDS

So, once we have forgiven the other person, where does this leave us? It means that the issue we had is no longer between us and the other person. If we have truly forgiven them, we can't bring up the issue again—it is now between that person and God. When we forgive biblically, we put the issue in God's hands and forget any notion of getting even.

To experience deliverance, we have to be honest with ourselves, with others, and with God. We have to be able to not only say the words "I forgive you" but also actually mean it. This may require that we continually pray and fast until the meaning of our words sink in. Why? Because when we take control of the outward life, we begin to take control of our inner desires and attitudes.

Freedom comes when we pray "thy will be done" each day to the Father and accept His will for our lives. Deliverance occurs when we take responsibility for our sins and sincerely repent and renounce our past mistakes. Deliverance occurs when we take responsibility for living in Christ and follow His direction. And we should always remember that we won't have the power to overcome our bondage until we make the choice to be free from bondage.

# YOUR ASSIGNMENT

*Checklist.* Check the last time you cried before God.

| Recently | Last Month | Last Year | Long Ago | Never |
|---|---|---|---|---|
| Wept over a lost person | | | | |
| Wept over a personal sin | | | | |
| Wept over a church problem | | | | |
| Wept over a family member | | | | |
| Wept over _____ | | | | |

*Repent of a hard heart.* If you haven't wept before God in a long time, maybe you need to repent of a hard heart. The harder your heart, the deeper you will need to repent. Maybe tears will come when you repent.

*Watch for action-related tears.* People cry when they lose something precious to them. The things that make you cry tell a lot about your value system. Make a list of the things that would make you cry if you were to lose them. This will help you understand your "spiritual temperature" before God.

*Seek God's prescription for breaking bondage.* You can't just ask God to take away your habit, because that's not the way God deals with freedom. Just as you developed your habit one act at a time, you must now take responsibility for each action you do. You must say no one step at a time. For more information on breaking bondage, read Neil Anderson, *The Bondage Breaker* (Eugene, OR: Harvest House Publishers, 2000).

*Make a daily commitment to be free from addiction.* Surrender your addiction once and for all to the Lord, and then commit to continually overcoming sin when temptation returns. Just as a member of Alcoholics Anonymous must recognize that he or she has a drinking problem and make a daily choice to stay sober, so you too must commit each day to being sober from your addiction before God. Note that at Alcoholics Anonymous meetings, a person often introduces himself by saying, "My name is ——, *and I am an alcoholic.*" When you recognize your weakness, you become stronger to overcome addiction.

*Fast to break addiction.* You may need to fast once a day for 40 weeks, or you may need to fast for 40 days. (However, don't go on this fast without great preparation.) Remember, God does not measure a fast by what goes into your mouth but by the things that come out of your heart.[3]

**Notes**

1. Elmer L. Town, *The Ten Greatest Revivals* (Ann Arbor, MI: Servant Publications, 2000).
2. The information in this section is based on material from Neil Anderson, *The Bondage Breaker* (Eugene, OR: Harvest House Publishers, 2000).
3. For more information on fasting, see Elmer Towns, *Fasting for Spiritual Breakthrough* (Ventura, CA: Regal Books, 1996).

# praise and worship

*For Yours is the kingdom and the power and the glory forever. Amen.*
MATTHEW 6:13

The final benediction of the Lord's Prayer is our opportunity to step back and acknowledge the awesome hand of God in our life. We recognize the rule of God's kingdom in our life and that He has the power to grant our requests, forgive our sins, and free us from bondage. When we say, "Yours is the glory," we offer a prayer of praise to God by giving Him all the glory and credit that He is due.

I must admit that I found this a very difficult chapter to write, mostly because I feel that I do not praise God nearly enough. Perhaps this is due in part to feeling that I do not know how to praise Him rightly. Or perhaps it is because I have not been grateful enough for all that God has done for me. But I think the main reason that I don't give adequate praise to God is because I just don't know enough about Him. He's infinitely greater than anything of which I can think or conceive. My praise is so *earthly*—and God needs *heavenly* praise. Any praise that I give to God is limited by my finite language and emotions. So how could I adequately praise an infinite God?

## ANGELIC PRAISE

In my mind, the type of praise that God needs is of the heavenly sort offered by angels. Now, when you think of angels, you probably picture beings dressed in white flowing robes with wings on their backs who fly here and there to deliver messages. Maybe you picture someone like the angel Gabriel who announced the birth of Christ to Mary (see Luke 1:26-38) or the two figures in shining garments that told Mary Magdalene and the other women that Christ had risen from the dead (see Luke 24:4-7). However, the primary reason why angels were created is to give glory to God. "And one [angel] cried to another and said: 'Holy, holy, holy is the LORD of hosts; the whole earth is full of His glory!'" (Isa. 6:3).

The praise that angels offer to God is far better than any praise that we as human beings can offer to God. For one thing, angels cannot sin, so their praise is not influenced by selfishness, duplicity or any tendency to wander from God—in other words, angelic praise is not influenced by any of the earthly desires that hamper our worship. Angels worship God constantly, while we only do it now and then. Angels worship God with "God-speech," while we are stuck with the limitations and stumbling of our human speech. And angels also know more about God than we do, so they can praise God with better knowledge, better wisdom and more exact understanding.

All of this brings up an important point: If God has a multitude of angels that can praise Him constantly with a form of worship that is purer and more heavenly than anything we could possibly achieve, why does He need us to praise Him at all?

## BLESS THE LORD

In Psalm 103, David writes, "Bless the LORD, O my soul; and all that is within me, bless His holy name" (v. 1). So, from this we learn that we should praise God from the bottom of our hearts and with our very being. But notice the word "bless" in this verse. What does *that* mean? To bless someone means to add some sort of value to his or her life here on Earth. We can bless people financially by giving them money, or materially by giving them something they need, or spiritually by giving them advice and counseling.

But how can we bless *God*? God doesn't need our money. He doesn't need any of the stuff we could give Him. He has all knowledge of His perfection, so there is nothing we could offer Him there. God needs absolutely nothing. So how can we bless or add value to God? The answer is very simple: We can't. We can't do anything to make God more than what He is.

However, when we "bless the Lord" we give God something that He cannot give Himself. It's a bit frightening to think that there is something that God *can't* do, but the truth is that God cannot worship or praise Himself. So, when we bless the Lord, we are adding the value to God that comes from redeemed souls who recognize His greatness and goodness for who He is and what He does for us.

When we praise God, we move out of ourselves and get closer to God than ever before. We move away from our prayers of petitions ("Give us this day our daily bread") and toward ones that focus solely on recognizing the glory and majesty of God. When we praise God, we don't ask Him to give us money, get us out of trouble, or provide us with anything. Our praise has nothing to do with us but everything to do with God. When we praise God, we do nothing but offer our selfless devotion to God as we exalt Him simply because of who He is.

## WHY PRAISE GOD?

So why must we praise God? One reason is simply because we are commanded to do so. The writer of Hebrews says, "Let us continually offer the sacrifice of praise to God, that is, the fruit of our lips, giving thanks to His name" (Heb. 13:15). Just as a grapevine gives forth the fruit of its grapes, so our mouth must give forth the fruit of our praise to God.

But another reason why we should praise God is what worshiping the Lord does for our hearts and minds. Each of us needs hope for something beyond ourselves. When we praise God for His infinite protection, we are lifted higher and closer to God's perfection than ever before. Praise is good for us because it keeps us from being pessimists. It keeps us from becoming bogged down in all the depressing circumstances of our everyday lives and focuses our attention on something greater than our present condition. Praise keeps us from being self-centered and negative.

Praise is also good for what it teaches us. When we learn to praise God, we quit being absorbed with ourselves and instead become absorbed with God. When we learn to quit praising our own efforts and focus on giving our praise to God—who alone *deserves* our praise—we begin to grow in grace and become more like Jesus Christ. And as we learn to do this more and more frequently, our relationship with God deepens. This is why the early disciples "were continually in the temple praising and blessing God" (Luke 24:53) and why Paul dedicated the book of Ephesians "to the praise of the glory of His grace" (Eph. 1:6).

Perhaps the greatest reason why we should praise God is that He *wants* our praise and worship. As Jesus stated to the Samaritan woman at the well, "The Father is seeking such to worship Him" (John 4:23). We should praise God simply because He wants it. God longs for us to long for Him.

We will never achieve the level of praise of that of the heavenly angels when they worship the Lord. Yet we can pray as David prayed when he wrote, "Let the words of my mouth and the meditation of my heart be acceptable in Your sight, O LORD, my strength and my redeemer" (Ps. 19:14). And since we will never be able to praise God with the words of angels, perhaps we can praise God with the words of Scripture. So let's allow the

Word of God (which is perfect) become our medium of praise. Let's use the Word of God so often that the words of Scripture become our own.[1]

## SO, WHAT IS PRAISE?

When Jesus was in Bethany at the house of Simon the leper, a woman poured an alabaster box of ointment upon Jesus' head. She did it as an act of love and worship, and Jesus said that throughout the history of the Church, her sacrifice would be recognized "as a memorial to her" (Matt. 26:13).

What happens when we attend memorial services such as the ones that are held each year on Veteran's Day or the ceremonies that are held to remember the events of September 11, 2001? What happens when we visit a site such as the Vietnam Memorial or the location where the Twin Towers fell in New York? Most likely, we remember what happened and adjust our lives accordingly—and often profoundly. So when we read this story of the woman who gave all that she had to Jesus, should we not remember all that Christ has done in our lives and adjust our worship and praise to Him accordingly?

Of course, when the woman poured the ointment on Jesus' head, there were some in the room who complained: "To what purpose is this waste?" (Matt. 26:8, *KJV*). There will be people in this world who will view our praise to God in much the same way. They will wonder why we are wasting our time going to church to worship God, or spending time in prayer, or giving our money to the Lord, or even why we are wasting our energy to sing songs of worship to God. Maybe you have asked this same question: "To what purpose is this waste?" If so, hear the rebuke of Jesus: "Why do you trouble the woman? For she has done a *good work* for Me" (v. 10, emphasis added).

So, what is praise? It is a *good work* that we pour out upon Jesus.

# YOUR ASSIGNMENT

*Bless the Lord.* We mentioned in this chapter that to "bless" some-one means to add some sort of value to someone's life. What types of things are you offering to "add value" to God? What can you do today to bless the Lord for who He is and for all that He has done for you?

*Become absorbed in God.* When we praise God, we take the focus off of ourselves and put it where it belongs—on God. Think of some of the negative things that are happening in your life. Now, think about something that God did in each situation to help you through that particular problem. Did He send a friend with an encouraging word? Was there anything positive that you learned from the experience? Think about ways that you will continue to focus on God in the days ahead, regardless of what life sends your way.

*Think of all the great things God does for you.* Make a list of all the things God has done for you, or just tell them audibly to God. When you thank God for all of these things, you begin to mag-nify Him. In Psalm 34:3, David tells us to "magnify the LORD . . . and let us exalt His name together." Consider the word "magni-fy" for a moment. Since it's impossible to magnify God because God cannot get bigger, what does it mean to magnify God? Well, think about people who wear reading glasses to see the small print of a newspaper. The glasses do not change the newspaper at all; they merely change the perception in the eye of the reader. In the same way, when we magnify the Lord, we do not make Him bigger, but rather magnify the Lord in our eyes. When we truly magnify the Lord, we grow in our understanding of Him and grow as believers in Him.

*Make a list of the many ways you can magnify God.* You magnify God in such ways as praying Scriptures, singing hymns or praise choruses, or even giving of yourself in some way. Maybe you're not growing as a Christian because you have not learned to truly magnify God. The more you magnify God, the more you grow. Doesn't God need to get larger in your perspective?

*Continually praise God.* David stated, "I will bless the LORD at all times; His *praise* shall continually be in my mouth" (Ps. 34:1). As you go through your day, consciously look for the little blessings that God sends your way and say a short prayer of thanksgiving to Him. (If you can't identify any of these blessings, reread the "Why Praise God?" section in this chapter.) How will you make focusing on the blessings and praising Him throughout your day part of your routine?

**Note**

1. For additional help on how to pray or praise God through the words of Scripture, see Elmer Towns, *Praying the Psalms* (Shippensburg, PA: Destiny Image Publishers, 2004). You can order this book at www.destinyimage.com or at www.elmertowns.com.

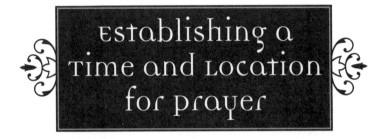

## establishing a Time and Location for prayer

*But thou, when thou prayest, enter into thy closet, and when*
*thou hast shut thy door, pray to thy Father which is in secret; and thy*
*Father which seeth in secret shall reward thee openly.*

MATTHEW 6:6, *KJV*

My eyes pop open. From between the warm sheets, I peek out at the digital alarm clock. The illuminated numbers tell me that it's 5:55 A.M. My muscles ache because I went to bed too late the previous night—I never feel like I get enough sleep. Yet even though my body is half asleep, my mind is already in gear. I begin to think about all the things that I have to do today.

I reach over and turn off the alarm. The alarm is set for 6:00 A.M. each morning, but for some reason my mind is programmed to awake a few minutes before it rings. I stretch my arms and legs and then fold the cover down to my waist. The rush of cool air awakens me. My mind and body are now on the same page. I'm ready to pray.

## SETTING A TIME FOR PRAYER

Some people tell me that they can't pray in bed. They claim that they fall back asleep if they don't get up out of their warm beds.

But once my eyes are open, my mind starts percolating and I'm ready to go. Instinctively, I begin to pray:

*Our Father who art in heaven* . . . may Your name be hallowed in my duties today . . . as Your name is hallowed in heaven.

*Your kingdom come* . . . may You reign in my life on Earth as You rule heaven.

*Your will be done* . . . let Your will be done in my studying . . . in my teaching . . . in my counseling . . . as Your will is done perfectly in heaven.

*Give me my daily bread* . . . give me physical strength for all of my needs this day.

*Forgive me my sins* . . . and forgive the consequences of my sins, including my actions and intent . . . and forgive others as You have forgiven me.

*Lead me not into temptation* . . . don't let sin overwhelm me, but give me victory today.

*Deliver me from the evil one* . . . protect me from physical and spiritual harm.

*For Yours is the kingdom* . . . I recognize Your sovereign control over my life.

*For Yours is the power* . . . I recognize Your ability to do all these things.

*For Yours is the glory . . .* I give You credit for every answer.

In Jesus' name, *Amen.*

Before I even get out of bed, I usually pray the Lord's Prayer in this manner. It takes all of about one minute. Now, I'm spiritually ready to begin my day. However, the prayer that I recite as I lie in bed is not part of my main prayer time—it is just my "waking up" prayer to get my day started right.

I turn the covers all the way back and slip on a pair of flannel sweat pants and a flannel sweat shirt (a bathrobe is not warm enough for me!). Going downstairs, I fix a pot of coffee—enough for me and my wife, Ruth—take my vitamin pills, and then jog out to the mailbox for the morning paper. Once that's done, I pour my coffee (no sugar, but a little cream) and then turn on the TV to *Headline News* to get the overnight events of the world. In about 15 minutes I've finished my coffee, read the paper, and am up to date on what's happening in the world.

Next, I pour two more cups of coffee (another cup for me to drink while I read my Bible and a cup for my wife). I head upstairs and wake up my wife, setting her cup of coffee on the nightstand along with the morning paper. When the weather is warm and my roses are blooming, I bring my wife a yellow Carolina rose to brighten her day.

Once Ruth is awake, I go into my office to begin my daily devotional time with God. I don't really have a set routine for these daily devotions—sometimes I begin by saying a prayer, sometimes I again recite the Lord's Prayer, and sometimes I just sing a few hymns to God. (If you have a hymnal, it's easy to find the prayer hymns—they're the ones that end with the "Amen" refrain.) I also sometimes just dig into a passage of Scripture.

This is my personal routine, which I have described so that you can get an idea of what a daily prayer time looks like. Perhaps you're a morning person who can jump out of bed and go straight into a prayer time with God. If that's your pattern, more power to you—keep going and don't let me interfere with your routine. Or maybe you're a night owl and have trouble forming sentences (much less prayers) in the morning—or maybe you just don't have time at that point in your day. If so, praying before you go to bed at night might be better for you.

Regardless of when you establish your prayer time, I encourage you to at least pray a short prayer (such as the Lord's Prayer) to God when you wake up. This will take just a few minutes and is a great way to begin your day by focusing on the Lord. Praying the Lord's Prayer while you are lying in bed is far better than not praying at all!

## SETTING A PLACE FOR PRAYER

Once you establish a regular prayer time, you will undoubtedly discover a favorite place where you will prefer to pray. In Scripture, this is known as a "prayer closet," but this seems to be a symbolic term means "private" or "quiet" place and not necessarily a place where we are commanded to pray. You may find that you enjoy praying on a balcony, on a sundeck, in a garden, at the kitchen table, or at the altar in a prayer chapel. You can pray any time or in any place.

As I mentioned, I meet God in my office each morning. However, when I was freshman in college, I knelt by my bed in the morning and evening. As a 19-year-old pastor of Westminster Presbyterian Church in Savannah, Georgia, I would go to a local wildlife park and pray in a secluded shelter that was out of sight from the public. Once there, I would tell God what I wanted to do in my church, and each day He would give me directions regarding what I should preach or how I should minister.

When I became pastor of Faith Bible Church in Dallas, Texas, my favorite place to meet God was on the top of a levee that separated the Trinity River from the community known as West Dallas. The night that I was called to the church, I went to the top of the levee to look out over the homes and dedicate myself to God. Although I didn't pray at the levee every day, I often returned to that place to pray over my "Jerusalem."

In the Bible, Moses had two places where he liked to pray: (1) the Tabernacle, because he experienced the presence of God there (see Exod. 40:34), and (2) on top of a mountain, because he also experienced the presence of God there (see Exod. 19:20). To Moses, wherever God was present was the perfect location for prayer.

Where is your favorite place to pray? My wife's favorite place is in the family room, where she likes to keep her Bible and notebook. We have an aunt whose favorite place was in the sunroom. And I also once knew a man who liked to retreat to his basement because it was quiet and private. Of course, maybe the best location to pray is wherever your feet happen to take you . . .

## PRAYER WALKING

In 1978, Ed Silvoso was diagnosed with myasthenia gravis, which is a disease that is similar to multiple sclerosis, in the same family of illnesses as Lou Gehrig's disease. Traveling from his home in Argentina for an experimental treatment in San Francisco, Ed planned to invest the rest of his short life in demonstrating that God could send revival in answer to prayer.

Ed had been involved in organizing crusades in some of the largest cities in South America. He organized massive crusades for Billy Graham and Luis Palau, Ed's brother-in-law, in Buenos Aires, Rio de Janeiro, and other great South American cities. Ed wanted to reach his home continent of South America, but he soon realized that it would not happen from the top down—that is, with big city crusades. He wanted to start at the bottom to show that revival begins when God's people pray.

When doctors told Ed in 1980 that he was "tenuously holding his own," Ed decided to return to his native Argentina. Once there, he began organizing people to walk around every block in the town of Rosario. He instructed them to go two by two, just as Jesus had sent out His disciples, and to pray for the people in every home they saw as they walked. Thus, *prayer walking* was born, which Ed defines as "praying on sight with insight."

After three months of prayer walking, Ed instructed his intercessors to go to the front door of each home with a notebook and tell the people, "We have been walking around this block every day to pray for you." Then Ed told his intercessors to ask the people they met, "How may we pray for you?"[1]

Unknown to Ed Silvoso, this was the beginning of a turnaround in the nation of Argentina. In 1980, only 1 percent of the population was evangelical Christian. By 2003, the Minister of the Interior for Argentina told me that evangelicals now represent 15 percent of that nation's population. In some of the states, more than 30 percent of the population was evangelical Christian. When I asked the Minister why this growth had occurred, he simply said, "Because evangelicals pray."[2]

Since the time that Ed Silvoso first coined the phrase "prayer walking," others have developed variations on Ed's ideas. Today there are *prayer journeys*, in which people walk from one destination to another while praying for specific needs along their routes. On several occasions, prayer pilgrims have journeyed to places in the world that were spiritually needy. Such was the case recently when a group of Christians walked the route of the Crusaders from Istanbul (the ancient city of Constantinople) to Jerusalem to mark the nine-hundredth anniversary of the Crusades.

And then there are *prayer excursions,* in which people journey to a location that is in need of prayer. During the late 90s and early twenty-first century, many Christians went on such prayer excursions to major cities within the 10/40 Window—the region of the word in which over 75 percent of cities with a population of over one million people are located. Since most of these cities are dominated by non-Christian religions, Christians take prayer excursions to these cities to pray for church planting, the growth of Christianity, and even for revival.

All of this is to point out that we may not even need a set location to pray—God can do miraculous things when we intercede for others as we walk down the street. Wherever God is present—be it in the streets of Rosario, Argentina, along the route of the Crusades, in the 10/40 Window, or in our own neighborhoods—incredible things can happen when we pray.

## LOCATION, LOCATION, LOCATION!

Some places just feel more comfortable than others, and there is nothing wrong with being comfortable or at ease when we enter the presence of God. Our favorite place to pray may be a bedroom, a den, or a private relaxing mountain retreat. We also should not ignore those locations in which we may have received a special blessing from God when we prayed on previous occasions. Each time we revisit such a place of prayer, we remember what God did for us, and the power of that memory builds our anticipation and makes us again desire to meet God. And isn't anticipation part of faith? Anticipating something can be the first step toward receiving the thing for which we are asking.

This is not to say that we always seek comfort or fond locations, for sometimes we will have to pick up our cross and follow Jesus. Sometimes the best prayers come from difficult places. As a college student at Columbia Bible College, I remember that the staff would always shut off the central heating system around 9:30 each evening. When I got ready to pray at 10:30 P.M. or later, the room was always cold. The challenge to me was to either keep praying in a chilly room or just forget the whole thing and jump into my nice warm bed and go to sleep. I chose to pray, even though it was not comfortable.

I believe that God delights in revealing Himself in certain locations. For some reason, Mount Sinai (also called Horeb), where God met Moses, was one of those places. On many subsequent occasions, God called Moses back to that mountain. Later, God also called Elijah to that same mountain (see 1 Kings 19:8-18). Jesus often met with God in the Garden of Gethsemane, which seemed to be one His favorite places to pray.

When we have a place where God has met us in the past, we'll find ourselves going back to that place. Eventually, it becomes one of our favorite places to pray. Then we practice what other people of God have done—we retreat to that same place to encounter God and meet with Him face to face.

# YOUR ASSIGNMENT

*Discover your prayer routine.* Determine what schedule works for you and follow it until it doesn't work any longer. There is no prescribed formula for establishing your daily devotions—there's only the principle of doing it faithfully each day. You can follow the routine I've outlined in this chapter or create one of your own.

*Look beyond the schedule to the relationship.* When you meet a good friend, there is probably no pattern to how the two of you talk—you just do it. Just as relationship is the glue that bonds you and your friend together, so prayer is the relationship that bonds you to God.

*Make the meeting imperative.* The key in any relationship is simply meeting with one another. Being present is even more important than what you talk about. It's the same way with meeting God every day—your relationship is more important than what you do first, or what you pray first, or the way you approach Scripture.

*Promise to meet the Lord each morning.* It's important to start the day by focusing on God. Since that's the most important relationship of the day, plan to be there each day. Just show up and you'll soon discover what to do when you meet with God.

*Make a list of places to pray.* Think through all the places you like to pray, and then make a list of those places where you felt the *presence of God.* Also include places on your list that beckon you to pray.

*Analyze your prayer locations.* As you analyze your prayer location list, write down the reasons why you enjoy praying in some places more than others. Usually you'll find one place that you'll enjoy more than others. Note this place and try to describe your feelings every time you return to pray in that spot. Make a decision to return to that place on a regular basis.

*When you don't feel like praying.* All of us face times and experiences when we don't feel like praying. It may be caused by sin, sickness, distractions or a number of other reasons. Determine that when these times unsettle your prayer life, you'll return to your prayer closet to meet with God there.

**Notes**
1. Ed Silvoso, *That None Should Perish* (Ventura, CA: Regal Books, 1994), pp. 31-35.
2. I journeyed to Mar de Plata, Argentina, to speak to approximately 10,000 Pentecostal-Charismatic pastors in a large basketball arena. That evening, the Minister of the Interior, along with the governor of the state, addressed the evangelicals, including other mayors and dignitaries.

## posture in prayer

*Then King David went in and sat before the LORD; and he said:*
*"Who am I, O Lord GOD? And what is my house,*
*that You have brought me this far?"*

2 SAMUEL 7:18

When I became a Christian on July 25, 1950, I was kneeling by my bed at approximately 11:15 at night. My hands were folded in prayer and I was looking up toward heaven through the open window next to my bed. I prayed, "Dear Lord Jesus, I have never done this before . . . come into my heart and save me."

I immediately sensed that my prayer had been answered. God gave me an immediate assurance that I was His child. I leaped to my feet and began punching my fist into the dark room as I silently praised God: "Praise God . . . Hallelujah . . . Amen!" My outward exaltation reflected the inner assurance that Jesus Christ had come into my heart.

I never believed that God heard my prayers *because* I was kneeling, folding my hands, or looking towards heaven. God heard my prayers because of the sincerity of my heart. However, for many years afterward, I always knelt when I had my private devotions—first by my bed in a dormitory room when I attended college and then later by a chair in my study at home. My outward posture always reflected my inner response to God. I knelt before God because He is my Master. I bowed my head in reverence to His majesty. I folded my hands as a symbol of petition.

However, at other times, I would open my hands to heaven in a symbolic gesture of receiving a gift from God. In times of complete abjection, I would stretch out with my face on the floor before God. These were the times when I would beg, plead and weep before the Lord.

Something happened when I was 68 years old. My ancient knees began to give out. They had traveled too far in life. When I knelt to pray, my kneecaps ached so much that I had difficulty keeping my thoughts on the Lord. So, I changed my posture. Now, I stand up in my office when I pray, or I pray as I walk through the house early in the morning. But I always felt guilty when I didn't kneel—it just didn't seem reverent to me to be standing or walking around while I prayed. So, I would go back to my office and kneel again, and soon the pain would return. And before long, I would again discover that I just couldn't keep my thoughts on the Lord— the sharp spasms of pain demanded my attention.

Finally, I realized one day that I was a legalist. I was forcing myself to kneel because of personal guilt and what I thought others expected me to do. I'd forgotten that God is more interested in the posture of my *heart* than He was in the posture of my *body*.

I began sitting down to pray, but even then I felt a twinge of guilt. However, God soon showed me a verse in the Bible that ultimately became the basis of my victory over bodily posture: "Then King David went in and *sat* before the LORD" (2 Sam. 7:18, emphasis added). Did you catch that last phrase, "before the LORD"? That's the key. It's not whether you stand or kneel or walk when you pray. The real issue is whether or not you are standing, kneeling or walking "before the LORD." So, as long as I keep God in my focus, I feel comfortable sitting while praying.

Now that we've determined that no single prayer posture is the "correct" one, let's take a look at some of the prayer postures that are given in Scripture.

# STANDING

Solomon is one of the greatest examples of a person in the Bible who would stand while he prayed: "Then Solomon stood before the altar of the LORD in the presence of all the assembly of Israel, and spread out his hands" (2 Chron. 6:12). Solomon's prayers were effective and became a model for all who like to stand as they pray. And there are many other suggestions in Scripture of people who stood while they prayed (see Matt. 6:5; Mark 11:25; Luke 18:11).

The psalms are filled with allusions to standing before God. Consider the following verses:

> Stand in awe, and sin not: commune with your own heart upon your bed, and be still (Ps. 4:4, *KJV*)

> You who stand in the house of the LORD, in the courts of the house of our God (Ps. 135:2).

> The boastful shall not stand in Your sight; You hate all workers of iniquity (Ps. 5:5).

> Who may climb the mountain of the LORD? Who may stand in His holy place? (Ps. 24:3, *NLT*).

Standing while praying has its advantages. Some people have told me that when they kneel, especially by their beds, they have a tendency to fall asleep. Some also have a tendency to fall asleep if they've had a hard day at work. However, people seldom fall asleep when they stand before God. Very few people can sleep standing up.

Let's also not forget those times throughout our day when we will want to say a casual or spontaneous prayer to the Lord while we are standing. Such was the case with Eliezer, the old servant of Abraham, who was commissioned to find a wife for Isaac. Eliezer traveled to Abraham's native land, and once there, he prayed, "O LORD God of my master Abraham, please give me success this day . . . Behold, here I stand by the well of water" (Gen. 24:12-13). And when the prophet Nehemiah stood before King Xerxes, he prayed, "O Lord, I pray, please let Your ear be attentive to the prayer of Your servant . . . and grant him mercy in the sight of this man" (Neh. 1:11).

## KNEELING

Apparently, when Solomon went in to dedicate the Temple, he began by standing before God but ended by kneeling before God:

> And so it was, when Solomon had finished praying all this prayer and supplication to the LORD, that he arose from before the altar of the LORD, from kneeling on his knees with his hands spread up to heaven (1 Kings 8:54).

There are many illustrations in Scripture of people who knelt when they prayed. Ezra fell to his knees when he prayed (see Ezra 9:5); Daniel knelt three times a day (see Dan. 6:10); Steven knelt as he interceded for his executioners (see Acts 7:60); Peter knelt when he prayed over Tabitha and raised her from the dead (see Acts 9:40); and Paul prayed with the elders, who knelt with him (see Acts 20:36).

Then there is the illustration of Jesus kneeling in the Garden of Gethsemane the night before He died. "And He [Jesus] was withdrawn from them about a stone's throw, and He knelt down and prayed" (Luke 22:41). If anyone didn't need to kneel, it was

Jesus—He is God! But by example, Jesus was instructing us to assume the right outward posture to reflect our inward attitude.

## BOWING

Bowing before the Lord is a symbol of respect and is actually something that we are commanded to do in worship: "Oh come, let us worship and bow down; Let us kneel before the LORD our Maker" (Ps. 95:6). In the Old Testament, God commanded the Israelites to not bow down to idols: "You must never worship or bow down to [idols], for I, the LORD your God, am a jealous God who will not share your affection with any other god!" (Exod. 20:5, *NLT*).

We are to give our allegiance and reverence to God by bowing to Him and Him alone. In fact, one of the symbols of unbelief and rejection of God is refusing to bow before the Lord. Paul told the Romans, "As I live, says the LORD, every knee shall bow to Me, and every tongue shall confess to God" (Rom. 14:11). He wrote something similar in his letter to the Philippians: "At the name of Jesus every knee should bow, of those in heaven, and of those on earth, and of those under the earth" (Phil. 2:10). And Paul noted to the Ephesians that he bowed his knees to the Father as an indication of his humble approach to God in prayer (see Eph. 3:14).

## PROSTRATION

The phrase "prostrating yourself before the Lord" basically means to lay facedown on the floor with your arms stretched out as an act of absolute submission to God. Prostration is the greatest posture of subjection to the Lord and is symbolic of one's desire to give the deepest reverence to Him.

When Israel sinned and God was about to judge them, Moses and Aaron laid prostrate before God (see Num. 14:5;

16:4). What motivated such an extreme posture? Perhaps Moses knew that the judgment of God for unbelief and disobedience was pretty severe—after all, he had spent 40 years in the wilderness because he murdered a man. When faced with the most extreme consequences, Moses assumed the most extreme position for intercession in prayer. After Job lost all his wealth and his children, he arose, tore his robe, shaved his head, and also "fell to the ground and worshiped" (Job 1:20). Job was stripped of everything in life, and his extreme suffering called for extreme worship. Job fell on his face before God.

When Elijah held a duel against the false prophets of Baal, Elijah prayed for fire to come out of heaven to burn up the sacrifice. "Hear me, O LORD," he cried. "Hear me, that this people may know that You are the LORD God" (1 Kings 18:37). God answered Elijah's prayer in an awesome way—fire fell from heaven and burned up the sacrifice. The false prophets were rounded up and—dispatched, so to speak.

This was a great answer to prayer, but Elijah wanted something more. Elijah wanted God to send rain from the heavens, for it hadn't rained in the land for three-and-a-half years. So Elijah assumed the extreme prayer posture of prostration before the Lord. He not only bowed himself before God but also put his head between his knees. "And Elijah went up to the top of Carmel; then he bowed down on the ground, and put his face between his knees" (1 Kings 18:42). I've tried this prayer posture a few times, and it's very difficult to keep your head in that position for very long. The blood rushes to your head and it's extremely uncomfortable.

Elijah wanted God to open up the heavens and bring forth a torrential downpour. Apparently, he kept his head between his knees long enough so that he could send his servant to look out upon the sea *seven times*. Each time, the servant came back and said there were no clouds in the sky (see 1 Kings 18:43).

Elijah kept on praying. Finally, the servant returned and told Elijah, "There is a cloud, as small as a man's hand, rising out of the sea!" (1 Kings 18:44). Elijah immediately knew that his prayer had been answered: "Hurry to Ahab and tell him, 'Climb into your chariot and go back home. If you don't hurry, the rain will stop you!'" (1 Kings 18:44, *NLT*). And what happened? "Sure enough, the sky was soon black with clouds. A heavy wind brought a terrific rainstorm, and Ahab left quickly for Jezreel" (1 Kings 18:45, *NLT*).

## FOLDING HANDS

What about folding your hands when praying? You've probably seen the famous painting that depicts Christ with hands folded in prayer. Did Christ actually do that, or is this an assumption of the artist? The traditional posture of bowing one's head with hands folded and eyes closed is found nowhere in Scripture. However, it has become an effective Christian tradition.

Scholars have made many suggestions about where this custom came from and when it began. Some say that this posture began as early as the "post-Exilic" period, when the Jews were taken captive by the Babylonians. Rabbinical writings relate how Rabbi Abba Ben Joseph (c. 280-352 B.C.) often prayed with his hands folded.

Some say the practice comes down to us from the priests who pronounced priestly blessing in the synagogue. After the priests stretched out their hands, they joined them together with the tips of the fingers of both hands touching. This represented unity; a division was shown when the priests spread apart their hands.

However, the source of folding hands is not important, and whether the practice is found in Scripture is not the issue. Posture is all about the attitude of our hearts. If we prefer to close our eyes, bow our head and fold our hands in the presence of God, we are showing reverence to the Lord. (Besides, it's just easier to not be distracted by everything around us if we close our eyes!)

# YOUR ASSIGNMENT

*Don't worry about your posture in prayer.* Your posture in prayer is not the most important thing when you approach God. It's the sincerity of your heart and your love for Him that counts, so put the emphasis on your relationship with God.

*Assume a posture of worship and respect.* However, don't approach God flippantly or disrespectfully. If you wrote a love letter on a piece of trash when better paper was available, what does that tell the other person about your love? If you came to see your loved one on a slow moving bus when faster transportation was available, what does that communicate to that person? Assume a bodily posture that best reflects your approach to God.

*Experiment with several postures in prayer.* The point of this exercise is not to experiment in order to experience different sensations—the goal is to determine what posture is best for you. Use the following chart to rate the various prayer postures:

|  | Comfortable/ Uncomfortable | Helpful/ Not Helpful | For Everyday/ For Occasions |
|---|---|---|---|
| Standing |  |  |  |
| Kneeling |  |  |  |
| Sitting |  |  |  |
| Folding hands |  |  |  |
| Bowing head |  |  |  |
| Bowing at the waist |  |  |  |
| Prostrate on floor |  |  |  |

The bottom line is that you won't necessarily be effective in prayer *because* of your posture, but your posture should always reflect the attitude of your heart.

# praying with others

*Again I say to you that if two of you agree on earth concerning anything
that they ask, it will be done for them by My Father in heaven.*

MATTHEW 18:19

My wife and I went through college by faith. If we had not prayed
together daily through all our difficulties, I don't know how we
would have made it. I earned one dollar per hour driving a
school bus, which was just enough to pay for our necessities.
There wasn't even a dime left over for a soda.

One evening, the only thing in our kitchen cabinet was a
can of tuna, so my wife made a tuna casserole. As we clasped
hands to thank God for the food, I prayed, "God, You know we
are broke. You know it's two days until payday. You know we are
willing to fast until we get money, but we ask you to please take
care of our needs."

As we finished praying, the laundry man came to the door.
Ruth met him at the door and said, "I'm sorry, there's no laundry today—we can't afford to have anything cleaned."

"Oh, I'm not here today to pick up your laundry," the man
replied. "A few months ago, your landlord asked me to pass
along 20 dollars to pay you for thawing some frozen pipes for
him. I had forgotten about it until today."

Some might say this was a coincidence, but Ruth and I believe
that it was the prayer that we said together that reminded the
laundry man he had 20 dollars to give to us.

# AGREEMENT IN PRAYER

Jesus made an incredible promise to us that if we agree with each other in prayer, the answer will come. "I say to you that if two of you agree on earth concerning anything that they ask, it will be done for them by My Father in heaven" (Matt. 18:19). The Greek word for "agree" used in the verse is the source for our word "symphony." Two people *praying in agreement* make beautiful music to God!

We can pray individually, but we must also learn to *pray in harmony* with others. When we pray together without agreement, it can be like screeching in the Lord's ears. And if you and your prayer partner are in disagreement, chances are that you are probably both wrong. We can solve much of our life's disharmony simply by agreeing with one another in prayer. When we agree together, God can answer.

So, what does agreement in prayer look like? What kinds of things are you and your prayer partner agreeing about? The following is a list of some of the items in which both of you should be in agreement.

## 1. Agree That God Can Answer Any Prayer

We should first agree that God does hear our prayers and has the ability to answer any prayer. "Is anything too hard for the Lord?" God asked when Abraham questioned whether his aging wife could truly bear a child (Gen. 18:14). When two people know and believe the promises of the Word of God, their faith can bring about answers. Note that the Greek word used for "ask" in Matthew 18:19 is *aiteo*, which simply means to request or call for an answer to a petition. There are many other words that are used in the Bible as a synonym for prayer (communion, fellowship, worship, praise, confession), but when God tells us to ask for what we need, we should do what He tells us—*ask*.

## 2. Agree That God Will Answer Our Prayers

The next step in the process is agreeing with our prayer partner that God *will* answer our prayers. This means that we must not only agree with each other but also with God. This means that both you and your prayer partner agree with the will of God.

## 3. Agree in Faith

Next, we must have faith that God will hear us when we pray according to His will. With this assurance, we can truly pray "in faith," believing in our hearts that God desires to answer our requests. When we pray such *prayers of faith*, we can be confident that God will answer our petitions even before we utter a word to our heavenly Father. We know it by faith. It is important to note here that regardless of whether we agree with others in prayer, God only answers our requests when His conditions have been met. These conditions can be summarized as follows:

- We ask sincerely
- We ask in faith knowing that we will receive an answer
- We continue asking
- We ask according to the Scriptures
- We ask in Jesus' name
- We make our requests in order to glorify the Father
- We ask according to the will of God
- We ask only after repenting for our sins

## 4. Agree on the Urgency of the Request

We should also agree on the urgency of the request and have unity in the intensity we feel. An urgent prayer is one that begins, "Lord, we need You right away—unless You intervene, there will be great tragedy." Only when we agree with our prayer partner that we desperately and urgently need an answer from God can we "two-pray" with fervency.

## 5. Agree to Be Completely Honest with Each Other

Prayer partners need to be completely open and honest with each other. Sometimes we can sense when the other person is holding back. At other times, we can be certain that our prayer partner is being 100 percent honest with us. Honesty is essential for creating agreement in prayer.

## 6. Agree to Confess All Sin

The Bible states that "all have sinned and fall short of the glory of God" (Rom. 3:23). We do not need to be perfect in order to have our prayers answered, but we do have to agree to not live in sin. To this end, we must agree to repent, confess and get rid of all known sins in our lives . . . and ask for forgiveness. "Now we know that God does not hear sinners; but if anyone is a worshiper of God and does His will, He hears him" (John 9:31).

## 7. Agree to Commit Our Prayers to God

Finally, we must totally commit our prayers to God and expect that He will answer. We shouldn't tentatively pray, "God, I'd sure like it if You could answer this prayer!" We also need to be careful not to hedge our prayers with loopholes that would allow us to change our minds or plans if things don't work out the way we think they should. Praying in this manner demonstrates a lack of sincerity on our part. If a young man asks a girl out on a date but then tacks on the condition, "If it doesn't rain" or "If things work out," this is not a sincere invitation. We need to seek out God with all of hearts and not hold back. "You will seek Me and find Me, when you search for Me with all your heart" (Jer. 29:13).

# YOUR ASSIGNMENT

*Make a list of the people with whom you are most comfortable praying.* After you complete your list, check off those individuals whom you feel are comfortable praying with you.

*Pray for potential partners.* Before you ask others to pray with you, pray that God will direct you to the right people. As you begin to pray for the people on your list, you'll discover those with whom you have a spiritual affinity.

*Talk with at least one person on your list about praying together.* Explain your desire to become a better intercessor and then tell that individual why you think he or she could help you learn more about prayer. Let that person know that you have been praying for him or her.

*Make an appointment (a time and place) to meet for prayer.* Begin by agreeing on a time and place to meet and then share Matthew 18:19 with that person. You may also want to tell him or her principles you've learned from this chapter. However, be careful not to let this become a one-way conversation, with you doing all the talking. Each of you should share the prayer burden.

*Determine if you have similar prayer burdens.* The glue that holds prayer partners together is a common prayer burden and desire. Commit to continue praying together if God is leading each of you in that direction.

# PART 2:

# STATIC ON THE LINE

## Devotional Readings on How to Pray in All Circumstances

Now that we have covered some of the basics on prayer, we can look at some of the issues and problems that often come up when we establish a prayer relationship with God. Similar to our relationships with friends and acquaintances here on Earth, when we establish a connection with God, we will typically go through a period of rough adjustments that will eventually lead to a deepening of the relationship. In this section, we look at some of the problems that we often encounter when we establish a prayer relationship with God, beginning with perhaps the most common problem—when we ask of God but don't receive.

# when we don't receive

*God does not hear sinners; but if anyone is a worshiper*
*of God and does His will, He hears him.*
JOHN 9:31

Many people say that God answers our prayers in three ways: *yes,*
*no* and *wait.* But I want to add a fourth way. Sometimes, I think
God says, "You've got to be kidding!"[1]

Whether or not this is actually the case, the thing that probably bothers each of us the most is that often we ask God to provide for us, but we don't receive anything in reply. Most of us
could certainly think of several prayers that God has not
answered in our life. So, how should we deal with this rejection?
If we ask God for something and He doesn't give it to us, what
should be our response? Should we rationalize that we didn't
have faith, that we didn't meet God's conditions, or that there's
sin in our lives?

## TESTING IN LIFE

We have to remember that if God answered our every request—no
matter how noble that request might be—there would be no war,
no crime, no sickness and no death. In other words, Earth would
be just like heaven. But that's not God's plan for this world.

When Adam and Eve sinned, they thrust the human race
into a battle against Satan. At times, the spiritual war does not

go well for us. God may throw us into battle to test our courage and see if we will remain obedient to Him. God allows us to face an enemy so that we will learn to depend on Him for the ultimate victory. God allows us to be defeated so that we will seek His presence during difficult times. Life is a test, and it's very important to score well on this exam.

If a sculptor doesn't chip away at the marble, he'll never create a beautiful statue. If a goldsmith doesn't throw the ore into the furnace, he'll never refine the gold to be fashioned into a thing of beauty. If the carpenter doesn't sharpen his tools, he'll never be able to cut the wood to make furniture for his house. "Dear brothers and sisters, whenever trouble comes your way, let it be an opportunity for joy. For when your faith is tested, your endurance has a chance to grow" (Jas. 1:2-3, *NLT*).

Have you ever prayed against the chisel as God chipped away at your greed, your selfishness, or your sin? Have you ever complained that God didn't answer your prayers for comfort as He heightened the flame that would make you as pure as gold? Have you ever prayed against the grindstone as God sharpened you for duty and service in His kingdom? Aren't you glad that the Divine Artist didn't answer your prayers in these instances but continued to sculpt your life into His beautiful creation? We want everything that we pray for every time, but sometimes we would be better served to seek God's will in the matter.

In difficult times of testing, we need to learn the lesson of *blind obedience* to God. We need to keep praying even when it seems as if nothing is happening and we feel like crying out to God, "Why do You hide Your face from me?" (Ps. 88:14). Sometimes God hides His face from us to test our obedience. He wants to know that we will follow Him blindly and continue to trust in Him, even when we don't get the results that we seek.

There are really two kinds of faith: *initiatory faith* and *continuing faith*. Initiatory faith is a very simple saving faith that puts us in touch with God. We begin our initial relationship with God by putting our trust—our faith—in Him and His Word. Continuing faith, however, is much more complex. It involves continually walking with God and believing in His love and grace even when it seems as if He is absent.

Think about it in terms of a relationship between a husband and a wife. When the two first meet and fall in love, they are in constant contact and form a relationship by placing an initial trust in each other. However, if the couple later experiences times away from each other, they must depend upon that initial trust and not doubt their love for each other—or the relationship will not survive. In the same way, when we feel separated from God, we need to walk in continuing faith and not doubt in the darkness what we've learned in the light. For God has promised, "I have loved you with an everlasting love" (Jer. 31:3).

When we cannot feel the presence of God, we must trust in His character. We must "trust in the LORD with all [our] heart and lean not on [our] own understanding" (Prov. 3:5). We must come to the place where you can say, "I may not understand what's happening or why I'm being tested, but I know that God loves me. I will choose to follow God in blind obedience."

## GOD'S PROMISES IN SCRIPTURE

It can certainly be frustrating when we read in the Bible that God promises to answer our requests, yet we still haven't received anything from Him. This is especially problematic when we read verses such as John 15:7, in which Christ states, "If you stay joined to me and my words remain in you, you may ask any request you like, and it will be granted!" (*NLT*). So if we can ask *any* request we like, why hasn't God answered our prayer?

Usually, the problem lies in our interpretation of these *seemingly* unconditional promises of the Bible. Notice that I said *seemingly*. The first rule of biblical interpretation is that the Bible interprets itself, so we can't just take any one promise or Bible verse by itself in isolation from the rest of Scripture. What may seem to be an *unconditional* prayer promise in one verse may actually have some other conditions placed upon it in other places in the Bible.

For example, John 14:14 states that if we ask for anything in God's name, He will grant our request. But Psalm 66:18 suggests that if we have not confessed the sin in our hearts, the Lord will not listen to our requests. The problem with having an impure heart is that it clouds our understanding of the will of God—and we then pray contrary to God's will. So it appears that one condition for God to grant our requests is that we must have a pure heart. Another part of Scripture elaborates on this point:

> The reason you don't have what you want is that you don't ask God for it. And even when you do ask, you don't get it because your whole motive is wrong—you want only what will give you pleasure (Jas. 4:2-3, *NLT*).

When the motives behind our requests are wrong, we're not being sincere with God and are not asking in faith.

Let's look at another example. Mark 11:24 states that whenever we ask for something, we need to believe that we will receive what we have requested. This seems to indicate that when our faith is sincere enough, we can expect God to grant any request we make. But sincerity alone is not enough—our prayers must also be tempered by biblical truth. God answers our prayers when we ask in faith according to the Word of God.

Consider the story in John 21 of the disciples when they went out fishing. After fishing all night long, the disciples still hadn't caught a single fish. When dawn arrived, they saw Jesus standing on the shore.

> [Jesus] called out, "Friends, have you caught any fish?"
> "No," they replied.
> Then he said, "Throw out your net on the right-hand side of the boat, and you'll get plenty of fish!" (vv. 4-6, *NLT*).

When the disciples obeyed the spoken words of Jesus, they received more fish than their nets could hold. The Word of Jesus, whether spoken or written, is the Word of God. It wasn't the disciples' sincerity that got them the fish; it was their obedience. They obeyed the spoken word of God, and they received.

## INSINCERE AND RIDICULOUS REQUESTS

Sometimes people ask for things that would go against the very nature of God if He were to answer those requests. I once counseled a lady who was praying for her unwanted pregnancy to go away. That's a prayer God won't answer. We cannot pray for yesterday to not have occurred.

Nor can we ask God to go against the laws of nature that He has established for this world. I once heard a preacher say, "I can do all things through Christ! I can even walk on air!" He honestly expected that God would make him fly. When he sincerely stepped off a chair in "faith," he fell straight to the ground. God works through His laws—and it's a rare occasion when He breaks those laws. One such occasion was when God made the sun and moon stand still so that the Israelites could defeat the Amorites. But even in this case, the Bible states, "And there has been no day like that, before it or after it" (Josh. 10:14).

The same is true of prayers that contradict the nature of time. A teenager may ask God to give him a strong body overnight, but his prayer will go unanswered. The laws of physiology state that muscular strength will only come over time as we exercise and eat a proper diet. Even if God does answer our requests immediately, it often takes time before we recognize that our petition has been granted. For example, if we ask God for money, He may answer that prayer immediately, but it will still require time for someone to write a check and mail it to us. We need to be cautious about praying for God to answer us *immediately*.

On other occasions, God may not answer our requests because He wants us to *do something*. We can pray for our friends to experience salvation, but until we take the initiative to speak with them about the gospel, it's a pretty insincere petition. Can we honestly ask God to draw people into our churches without first inviting them to come?

Sometimes God doesn't answer our prayers because we ask for things that are contrary to His big picture. We ask for things that would harm us or for God to give us things that might not be in our best interest. Before I met my wife, I dated several other girls in Bible college. I thought that each girl was beautiful, spiritual and would make a great wife for me. I prayed with short-sightedness, asking God to give me the heart of each girl. God didn't answer. Now, after being married for 52 years to the perfect mate, I praise God that He didn't answer those prayers!

Some prayers are not answered because they fall within the "mystery of God"—God's unknown purpose. When I pray for sick people, some get well, but others die. None of us understands why this happens. If we understood all of God's mysteries, we would always pray according to God's will—but we don't, so we can't. "For now we see in a mirror, dimly, but then face to face. Now I know in part, but then I shall know just as I also am known" (1 Cor. 13:12).

# YOUR ASSIGNMENT

*Think about some prayers that you're glad God didn't answer.* It's often humorous to look back on our past requests and realize why God didn't answer our prayers. With hindsight, we can often realize just how foolish some of those prayers were, or what a pickle we'd be in if God had decided to answer our blind requests. Make a list of those preposterous requests, and then laugh at yourself. Not only will you enjoy the moment, but you might also grow spiritually as you learn not to make those requests again.

*Write a list that will make you cry.* Think about some of the times when you asked God for something out of improper motives or selfish desires. Maybe you asked for something that ultimately brought you sorrow or hardship. You'll be convicted when you write out these items, but you'll also learn what you shouldn't request in the future.

*Ask for blind faith.* There is a reason why God doesn't answer certain requests, but we don't always understand those reasons. Ask for faith to trust in God when He doesn't answer your requests. You'll then accept His answer as the best answer.

*Read the stories of a few people in the Bible who went through a time of testing.* Some good examples include:

- Job, who endured great suffering (see Job 1–2)
- Joseph, who was sold as a slave to Egypt and ignored in prison (see Gen. 37–40)
- Moses, who spent 40 years in Sinai before God called him to deliver Israel (see Exod. 1–4)
- David, who spent 13 years running from Saul (see 1 Sam. 18–24)

*Study the character of God.* The following Scriptures will help you understand the character traits of God. Whenever you can't feel God's presence or doubt His love for you, read these Scriptures so that you can continue to walk in faith with the Lord.

| Character Trait | Scripture |
|---|---|
| **Omnipotent (All-Powerful)** | Gen. 18:14; Jer. 32:27; Job 42:2; Pss. 19:1-6; 33:6-12; 135:5; Matt. 19:26; Mark 14:35; Luke 1:34-37; Rom. 1:20; 4:18-21; 1 Cor. 6:14; Eph. 1:18-21; 3:20-21; Rev. 4:11; 5:11-12 |
| **Compassionate** | Exod. 33:19; Pss. 86:15; 103:13; 145:8-9; Lam. 3:22; Micah 7:18-19; Matt. 9:36; 14:14; 15:32; 18:27; 20:34; Mark 1:41; 6:34; Luke 1:78; 7:13; 10:33; 2 Cor. 1:3; Jas. 5:11 |
| **Eternal** | Deut. 33:27; Pss. 29:10; 33:11; 48:14; 102:27; Isa. 40:28; 44:6; 57:15; Dan. 4:35; Rom. 1:20; 1 Tim. 1:17; 2 Pet. 3:8; Rev. 1:8; 4:8-11 |
| **Faithful, Trustworthy** | Exod. 15:11; 36:6; Lev. 11:44; Deut. 7:9; 32:4; Josh. 21:45; 1 Sam. 2:2; Pss. 5:4; 18:30; 25:10; 33:4; 86:15; 91:4; 92:15; 100:5; 117:2; 119:89; Prov. 9:10; Isa. 6:3; Lam. 3:22-23; Luke 1:49; John 17:11; 1 Cor. 10:13; 2 Thess. 3:3; Heb. 10:23; 1 John 1:9; 1 Pet. 1:15; Rev. 4:8; 6:10 |
| **Impartial** | Deut. 10:17; 2 Chron. 19:7; Job 34:19; Acts 10:34; Rom. 2:6; 10:12; Gal. 2:6; Eph. 6:9; Col. 3:25; 1 Pet. 1:17 |
| **Incomprehensible** | Job 11:7-9; Eccles. 3:11; Isa. 40:12-14,25-26; 55:8-9; 1 Cor. 2:16 |
| **Unchanging, Immutable** | 1 Sam. 15:29; 1 Kings 8:56; Job 23:13; Pss. 33:11; 102:26-27; Isa. 14:24; Eccles. 3:14; Mal. 3:6; Heb. 6:17-18; Jas. 1:17 |

## Note

1. Dave Earley, *The 21 Most Effective Prayers of the Bible* (Uhrichsville, OH: Barbour Publishing, Inc., 2005), p. 8.

# when we feel abandoned

*Sometimes I ask God, my rock-solid God, "Why did you let me down?*
*Why am I walking around in tears, harassed by enemies?"*
PSALM 42:9, *THE MESSAGE*

Have you ever had a conversation with a friend where it didn't seem as if the message was getting through? Maybe it's a feeling that you get when you look your friend in the eyes and notice that her eyes don't light up when you speak. The blank expression you receive makes you feel as if you are talking to a brick wall. Instead of your friend being a sounding board to bounce an idea back to you, your words just bounce off and fall lifeless to the floor.

Each of us has felt this way about God at some point in our lives. Like talking to an unresponsive friend, we seek God in prayer and come to Him with our requests, but it feels as if those petitions have just fallen on deaf ears. As mentioned in the previous chapter, because we don't understand all of the mysteries of God, we don't always understand why our prayers have seemingly gone unanswered. And this can certainly lead us to believe that we have been forsaken and abandoned by God.

## ABANDONMENT AND DOUBT

Sometimes we feel forsaken because we have actually been deserted. Maybe we have experienced some hard times through the loss of a job, a personal illness, or other crisis and no one has come to rally around us. We feel utterly abandoned and alone, and our doubts and questions throw us off balance. Like Job—who certainly understood what it meant to be abandoned by God—we cry, "God, where are You?"

When we feel forsaken, we want an answer. Any answer! Even if God were to say no, that would at least give us the assurance that He heard us. Sometimes it just seems as if God is not there when we pray. So what happens when we feel *forsaken*? Well, we doubt whether God really loves us. We question whether He hears us—and whether He even exists.

Such was the case with Thomas, the doubting disciple. On resurrection day, Jesus appeared to the disciples, but Thomas was not there (see John 20:24). And where was he? Well, like the other disciples, Thomas ran away and hid when Jesus was arrested. We can imagine the disciples hiding in closets, in caves, or among the trees in the forest. We may give Peter a hard time for denying Christ, but at least he didn't flee the scene—he sat in the courtyard where Jesus was being tried (see Matt. 26:69).

Apparently, Thomas ran farther away and hid himself deeper than all the rest—so far that he was completely out of reach for a while. So on resurrection day, when Jesus appeared to 10 of the disciples and "showed them His hands and His side" (John 20:20), the disciples had a chance to examine carefully the wounds, and they understood what they saw (the Greek word "show" used in this verse is *eidon,* which means not only "looking" but also "understanding" what one is looking at).

During the next week, the disciples told Thomas that they had seen the Lord. But because Thomas hadn't seen Christ and examined His wounds, he was skeptical. "Unless I see in His hands the print of the nails, and put my finger into the print of the nails, and put my hand into His side, I will not believe" (John 20:25). Thomas felt shut out and abandoned. No wonder he was a doubter!

Are you like Thomas? Do you feel deserted and left out of God's promises? Do you feel that God has *forsaken* you and doubt that He will keep His promises to you? Do you long for Jesus to say, "Reach your finger here, and look at My hands; and reach your hand here, and put it into My side. Do not be unbelieving, but believing" (John 20:27)?

It's a lonely feeling to be abandoned. Perhaps David expressed this feeling best when he exclaimed, "My God, I cry in the daytime, but You do not hear; And in the night season, and am not silent" (Ps. 22:2). But instead of allowing our feelings to lead us to doubt the love of God, we should ask a deeper question: "God, why don't You care about me?" We should pray with the psalmist, "Why have You forgotten me? Why do I go mourning?" (Ps. 42:9).

## HAVE WE TRULY BEEN ABANDONED?

Each of us has at some time felt abandoned by God, and we may have even doubted God's love for us during these times. But has God really forsaken us?

Maybe the truth is that God hasn't forsaken us, but that we have forsaken Him. It's kind of like the little boy who runs outside and wonders where his mother has gone. She is sitting at the kitchen table—but the little boy is so busy looking everywhere else that it doesn't dawn on him that he needs to come *inside* to find his mother. When we feel abandoned by God, we need to make sure that we are looking for Him in the right places.

Or maybe the reason why we haven't heard from God is because we block Him out with our chatter. God may stop talking to get us to be quiet. When we become still before God and listen for His voice, we have a better chance of hearing Him. Only when everything is quiet can we sincerely search our hearts and uncover anything that might be blocking our connection with the Lord—such as any sin that we might have buried there.

In a similar manner, God may "forsake" us so that we will examine our motives to determine if we are praying for the wrong reasons. As mentioned in the previous chapter, when the motives behind our requests are wrong, we're not sincere with God and are not asking in faith. God's absence may be an indication that He wants us to examine our hearts.

Of course, our feelings of abandonment might also stem from wrong ideas about God. Maybe we think that God will always answer any prayer the way we want at any time. As we read in the last chapter, this is not the case. We cannot control God, and He doesn't always answer just because we call. Sometimes God knows that we need to spend a lonely night by ourselves so that we will draw closer to Him.

## FINDING GOD

How do we reconnect with God when we feel that He has abandoned us? Where do we begin to look for God? What can we say when we experience static on the line? One good place to begin looking is in the Word of God. In 2 Timothy 3:16, Paul writes:

> All Scripture is inspired by God and is useful to teach us what is true and to make us realize what is wrong in our lives. It straightens us out and teaches us to do what is right (2 Tim. 3:16, *NLT*).

The word used for "inspired" in this verse literally means "God-breathed." God breathes His presence into the Bible, so when we read His Word, we expose our minds to God's presence. When we discover God in the pages of the Bible, we will no longer feel forsaken.

What should we pray when we feel forsaken? Maybe we should start by noting what we *shouldn't* say. We must be careful not to offer a prayer of complaint in which we blame God for leaving us. "But to you I have cried out, O LORD, and in the morning my prayer comes before You. LORD, Why do You cast off my soul? Why do You hide Your face from me?" (Ps. 88:13-14). We sometimes blame God for forsaking us when *we* are to blame.

Rather than blaming God, why not ask Him to speak to us? As the psalmist wrote, "Do not keep silent, O God of my praise!" (Ps. 109:1). Like the little boy who is looking for his mother, we need to exclaim, "I'm lost!" and then cry out for the presence of God. There's nothing so cleansing as confessing these two simple words to God. We need to ask God to speak to us, and then keep quiet and *listen* for what He says. We also need to remember that our prayers are best heard when we *surrender everything* to God.

## THE PRAYER OF ABANDONMENT

We all need to learn the prayer of abandonment. When Jesus was preparing Himself to do His Father's will and suffer death on the cross, He understood the awful consequences before Him. He understood that He would be tortured, mocked and abused by His accusers. He realized that in a few short hours He—who had lived a sinless life—would be taking on all the depth of vulgarity and iniquity that the cross represented. Worst of all, Jesus understood that He would be utterly alone as He died on the cross, for God the Father, being holy, cannot endure the presence of sin. It's no wonder that the night before His death, Jesus prayed, "Father, if it is Your will, take this cup away from Me" (Luke 22:42).

It is clear that Christ honestly didn't want to endure the suffering that was in store for Him and that He wanted His Father to take this burden from Him. We should all be grateful that this prayer wasn't answered! If God had chosen to spare His Son, our sins wouldn't have been forgiven. And as a result, we would have to face the judgment of God, for "There is none righteous, no, not one" (Rom. 3:10).

But Jesus yielded His will to the Father, saying, "not my will, but Yours, be done" (Luke 22:42). He went to the cross, suffered and died for our sins. And as the heavens turned black and the sun hid its face, Jesus was left utterly abandoned and alone. He cried out in agony, "My God, My God, why have You forsaken Me?" (Mark 15:34).

Sometimes we feel abandoned when God calls us to go into a difficult situation or to part with someone or something that we truly love. It's like the Christian couple who falls in love in college but finds out that God has different purposes for their lives—he has been called to the mission field overseas, while she has been called to stay and go into business. What must they do? Neither can give up their calling for the other person, because then they won't be in the center of God's will. So they must pray the difficult prayer of abandonment: "Lord, Your will be done, not ours."

In instances such as this, it is especially hard to pray the prayer of abandonment because the thing we are giving up will never be returned to us. When the brokenhearted girl surrenders to the will of God and watches her boyfriend board the plane for the mission field, she knows that she will never get him back. That's tough to handle. She will probably feel abandoned by God and doubt His love for her. But at such times, we need to trust the wisdom of God and that He will give us His grace so that we can live with the results.

## THE LESSON OF ABANDONMENT

In 2 Corinthians, Paul writes that he believed he was praying for the perfect will of God when he asked the Lord to remove the "thorn" from his flesh. We don't know exactly what this thorn represented in Paul's life, but Paul prayed three times that God would remove it (see 2 Cor. 12:7-8). But God didn't answer that prayer. Paul had to abandon his physical comfort and accept the consequences of the thorn in his flesh. Yet through the experience, Paul learned an important lesson: If he surrendered to God, the grace of the Lord would be sufficient to care for him. The Lord told Paul, "My grace is sufficient for you, for My strength is made perfect in weakness" (2 Cor. 12:9).

Sometimes God asks us to abandon happiness for what appears to be loneliness. Sometimes He asks us to abandon physical comfort for physical pain or torture. Why does God require this of us? Because God requires *death* before He brings forth *life*. The Bible says, "Unless a grain of wheat falls into the ground and dies, it remains alone; but if it dies, it produces much grain" (John 12:24). Abandonment sometimes leads to the death of our pleasure . . . or our comfort . . . or our ambitions . . . or even our immediate happiness.

But God doesn't leave us in a state of turmoil when we abandon ourselves to His will. When we abandon our desires to pursue those of God, we turn from our feelings of self-love and self-protection and move toward divine love and divine worship. It is then that we get a new desire for living. It's in that transformation that we find a new desire to worship God. When we die to our selfish plans, we become like the wheat that dies in the soil. Through death to self, we slowly begin to grow and become fruit unto the glory of God.

When we relinquish the desires of our heart and submit to God's will, we crucify our will to Christ and allow God to transform our lives. This is what Paul means when he states, "I have been crucified with Christ; it is no longer I who live, but Christ lives in me" (Gal. 2:20). We loosen the grip on our earthly pursuits and instead focus on the things of God's kingdom—and become more like Christ in the process. When we pray, "Not our will, but Yours, be done," we receive something that will last: the indwelling of Christ in our lives.

This may seem a bit harsh. Does God really want us to eradicate our will? Not at all—when we pray, "not our will, but Yours," we are talking about *surrendering* our wills, not destroying them. Our will represents our power to make decisions in life. When we eradicate our wills, we become like pieces of paper blown down an empty alley that follow the dictates of the wind, with no backbone . . . no determination . . . no purpose in life.

God does not want to destroy our power of choice; He wants to transform it. He wants to transform it into something good so that we will choose to pursue the will of God. In the same way that our will must die to selfish ambition, it must live again to the new resurrection life of Jesus Christ. The prayer of abandonment must always lead to the prayer of transformation: "Lord, I give my life to You. Now transform me into the image of Jesus Christ." This only occurs when we move beyond abandonment and are transformed to love and obey God.

## WHEN DARK TIMES COME

Dark times will come in each of our lives when we will feel forgotten by God and completely alone. When we find ourselves in such dark situations, we need to remember to keep doing the things that we learned to do in the light—listen for God's voice, read the Bible, worship the Lord, and carry on the commands that He has given. We also need to remember that God never intended these dark times to be permanent. Just as the day is divided into periods of light and dark, we will often encounter darkness on our spiritual journeys—but we can be assured that the daylight will come again.

We must also remember that God accomplishes many things in the darkness of night. The coolness of the night allows the root systems of plants to grow. The dew falls to refresh the leaves of the plant when there is no sun. Just as God has intended our physical bodies to get refreshment from sleep, we must realize that God has a purpose for our night seclusion—and we must learn what those purposes are.

God may have brought some confusing circumstances into our lives that resulted in deep feelings of frustration. We may feel abandoned and alone. But realize that "all things work together for good to those who love God" (Rom. 8:28). Even the frustration of feeling forsaken can be good if it makes us search for the Lord. For just as when the little boy cries out "I'm lost" and his mother finds him and wipes away his tears, our frustrations of feeling forsaken may lead us into the warm embrace and comfort of God Himself.

# Your Assignment

*List and analyze some times of frustration.* Make a list of some times when you were frustrated and didn't feel the presence of God. Now analyze the list and ask yourself the following questions:

- What caused my frustration?
- How deep was the frustration?
- What did the frustration teach me?

After you answer the above questions, write out what you learned.

*Memorize verses of Scripture about overcoming frustration.* Here are a few good passages to memorize:

Whenever I am afraid, I will trust in You (Ps. 56:3)

We know that all things work together for good to those who love God, to those who are the called according to His purpose (Rom. 8:28).

Rejoice in the Lord always. Again I will say, rejoice! (Phil. 4:4).

*Look in your heart.* Is there anything in your heart that stands between you and the will of God? If so, do the following:

1. Acknowledge that there is a barrier between you and God. Recognizing that such a disconnect exists in your relationship is the first step to resolving it.
2. Ask God for the strength to see the barrier as it is and to pray honestly. Your prayers won't get through until you mean it.

3. Write in your prayer journal what will happen if you don't abandon the barrier between you and the will of God.

*Tell God how you feel.* If you are frustrated or feel abandoned by God, tell Him how you feel. Ask Him to help reveal the barriers that may be causing a disconnect in your relationship and reveal His purposes to you.

*Determine to always trust in God.* Sometimes faith in God requires blind obedience. So determine every day that while you may not know why God seems to be turning His face from you, you will believe in your heart that God always has your best interests in mind.

# when we are desperate

*This poor man cried out, and the Lord heard him,
and saved him out of all his troubles.*

PSALM 34:6

Sometimes situations come into our lives that make us *desperate* for God. This may be a situation in which we experience a crisis and need the immediate power of God—when all that we have time to do is cry out to God for help. Or this could be a situation in which we experience a crisis in our spiritual lives that makes us hungry for God—times when we feel empty, spiritually weak and starved for fellowship with God. In this chapter, we'll discuss such *prayers of desperation.*

## HELP, LORD! I'M SINKING!

Matthew 14:24-30 gives us an example of a desperate prayer: Peter was in the ship with the disciples when a great storm arose that threatened their lives. The disciples pulled on the oars as hard as they could but made no headway toward the shore. Then, through the blowing wind, they saw someone walking toward them—on the water! "It's a ghost!" the disciples cried out in fear.

Of course, it was not a ghost, but Jesus Christ who was coming to their aid. "It's all right!" Jesus said. "It is I; do not be afraid" (v. 27). Peter, a man of action, immediately responded, "Lord, if it is You, command me to come to You on the water" (v. 28).

"Come!" was Jesus' simple response.

So Peter immediately jumped out of the boat and began walking on the water—something a human had never done. At first, his eyes were fixed on Jesus, and he remained on the surface of the waves. But then Peter did something wrong: He took his eyes off Jesus. And when "he saw that the wind was boisterous, he was afraid; and beginning to sink he cried out saying, 'Lord, save me!'" (v. 30).

This was a time for *desperate prayer*. Peter was sinking fast in a stormy sea and didn't have time to form a proper petition to his Lord. He didn't have time to confess the mistake that caused him to sink. He didn't even have time to think about what he was doing. All Peter could do was cry out to God because he was scared to death. He knew that the Lord is "a very present help in trouble" (Ps. 46:1) and that Jesus had the power to save him.

My pastor often says, "There are more bad days than good days." We will all encounter situations in which the threat is so immediate and overwhelming that all we will be able to do is cry out to God in desperation. Like Peter, we will see the storm raging around us and feel the water begin to rise, and the first thing that will come to our minds is to turn to God for help. Desperate prayers will spring from our desperate hearts. "Let us therefore come boldly to the throne of grace, that we may obtain mercy and find grace to help in time of need" (Heb. 4:16).

## LEARNING TO TRUST GOD IN TIMES OF TROUBLE

Sometimes, God will allow us to encounter trouble in our lives. Why? Because He wants to get our attention and help us learn to call on Him in our time of need. He wants to draw us into His presence so that we will abide in Him and worship Him. "In the time of trouble He shall hide me in His pavilion; in the secret place of His tabernacle He shall hide me" (Ps. 27:5). If you haven't been seeking

God's presence and haven't been worshiping Him, watch out! Situations may be on the way that will draw you closer to God.

In the Old Testament, King Asa, one of the godly kings in Judah, encountered a situation in which he experienced the same "sinking feeling" as Peter. An Ethiopian named Zerah was attacking Judah with an army of thousands. Asa knew that he was in trouble and that he didn't have the manpower to stand against the Ethiopian onslaught. So what did Asa do? "Asa cried out to the LORD his God" (2 Chron. 14:11).

Asa cried what all people in trouble cry: "Help!" Asa prayed to the Lord, "Help us, O LORD our God, for we rest on You, and in Your name we go against this multitude. O LORD, You are our God; do not let man prevail against You!" (v. 11). Asa began his prayer of desperation by asking God to defend him against the multitude of Ethiopians, but by the end Asa noted that the Ethiopians were actually fighting against God.

After God's people won the battle, the prophet Azariah reminded Asa that whenever Israel was in trouble in the past and "turned to the LORD God of Israel, and sought Him, He was found by them" (15:4). Azariah told Asa that the Lord would continue to be with the Israelites as long as they were on the side of the Lord and followed His commands. God was teaching His people that when they called on Him in their times of desperation, He would answer the call and deliver them from their enemies.

The secret to having our prayers answered by God is to put our complete trust in Him. When we're absolutely terrified because there is no one to help us and nothing to prevent us from being destroyed—when all hope is gone—we tend to cry out sincerely with our whole hearts and trust in our heavenly Father. Fear strips away all pretences and enables us to cry out in sincerity from the depth of our heart. In desperate conditions, we can't trust anyone else or anything else besides God, because everything else has failed. It is in these moments that God has our full attention.

Of course, in order for God to deliver us, we have to believe in our hearts that He can save us. In the Bible, two blind men followed Jesus, desperately crying, "Son of David, have mercy on us!" (Matt. 9:27). The men *cried out* because they wanted to make sure that Jesus heard them; they cried out *desperately* because they suffered the limitations of blindness every waking second and wanted Christ to heal them.

Jesus heard their pleas, but instead of immediately healing them, He first asked them an interesting question: "Do you believe that I am able to do this?" (v. 28). Jesus already knew the blind men desperately wanted to see, but He didn't know if they *believed* that He could do it. He didn't know if they believed that He was the Son of God. So Jesus waited for their affirmation before He answered their petition.

## SPIRITUAL DESPERATION

In the Bible, two priests were walking toward Jerusalem. They had been in a land of exile far away and their greatest passion was to return to the Promised Land and worship God in the Temple. As the priests walked, they saw a young deer being chased by dogs and hunters. As the fawn ran for its life, it stopped just long enough to take a life-saving drink of water in a mountain stream. The scene captured the imaginations of the two priests, who wrote, "As the young deer being chased stops long enough for a drink of water, so my soul pants for God" (Ps. 42:1, *ELT*).

Have you ever felt this kind of hunger for God? Have you ever experienced a hunger so intense that you almost forgot how to pray? Or have you ever had your words just gush from your mouth and felt that your emotions were chaotic?

That's what it is like when we experience a *spiritual hunger* for God. When our souls are empty . . . and we're spiritually weak . . . we become so desperate for fellowship with God that we forget about everything else. As in moments of crisis, we don't begin our prayer time with praise and worship or a time of confessing our sins to God—we simply pour out our souls to our Lord (see Ps. 62:8).

It's like setting a meal in front of a starving man. A starving man will tear into the food without any thought for manner or protocol. He'll stuff his mouth with the first thing within reach. He won't think about using knives, forks or any utensils—he'll use his fingers. He'll swallow without chewing. A starving man doesn't think of others and worry about appearances. He just cares about satisfying his hunger.

Jesus is the Bread of Life and can satisfy all of our hunger. In John 6:35, Jesus says, "I am the bread of life. He who comes to Me shall never hunger again." Jesus is the Water of Life and can quench even our most desperate thirst. "If you are thirsty," Jesus tells us, "come to me! If you believe in me, come and drink! For the Scriptures declare that rivers of living water will flow out from within" (John 7:37-38, *NLT*).

We don't have to be fancy or proper. If we're hungry and thirsty for God, all we have to do is pray.

## JUST A TASTE

But what if we're not feeling hungry for God? What if we the kind of person who can go days without thinking about God? Well, we don't have to be discouraged when we don't feel a desire to pray. The very fact that we are *now* thinking about praying will build up our hunger for God. We will then want prayer and intimacy with God.

Actually, the two things work together. Prayer is hunger for God, and having a genuine hunger for God is the beginning of prayer. Our genuine *desire* to know God is an actual prayer, and genuine prayer makes us hungry for God. Genuine prayer is *God-hunger.*

The psalmist writes, "Taste and see that the LORD is good" (Ps. 34:8). Sometimes the secret to hunger is taste. If we don't have a spiritual appetite for God, then maybe we can get a "taste" for the Lord—pray just a little—and we'll get an appetite for more. This always happens to me when I'm in the ice cream shop—the attendant uses one of those small taste spoons to tempt me with some new flavor and after one taste, I'm hooked. I buy a double scoop cone. Isn't that one of the functions of taste? When we taste a little bit, it makes us want more.

One way to develop a hunger for God is to read a few verses from the Bible. The Word of God will be sweet to our taste (see Ps. 119:103). We turn our face to Jesus to seek His presence and taste that the Lord is gracious (see 1 Peter. 2:3). Like the pleasant first taste of that ice cream cone, we'll hunger for more.

Tasting usually tells us what's to follow. When I sit down to a steak, I cut off a little bite—just a taste. That tells me if it's cooked the way I like it. The first taste excites my taste buds for more. In the same way, when we sincerely talk to God—and He talks with us—we will naturally want more and more fellowship with Him. Some people have difficulty finding time to pray, but I'm the opposite. When I taste the presence of God, I have difficulty breaking away.

God desires to have fellowship with us. When we come into His presence, we will find Jesus saying, "I have meat to eat that ye know not of" (John 4:32, *KJV*). As we approach God and knock on heaven's door, we will find Jesus knocking at the door of our hearts. "Behold, I stand at the door and knock. If anyone hears My voice and opens the door, I will come in to him and dine with him, and he with Me" (Rev. 3:20). Just as two people seek out one another for fellowship, God is seeking fellowship with us as we seek fellowship with Him.

# Your Assignment

*Memorize verses.* When desperate times come, you won't have time to look up Bible verses or study the Scripture. If you memorize Scripture, it'll be there to help you in times of distress. Memorize Pss. 27:5; 34:6; 46:1; 56:3; 121:1; 2 Chron. 14:11; Matt. 9:28.

*Ask God to prepare you for any future emergency.* Technically, you can't prepare for an emergency, but you can get the right mental attitude to deal with an emergency when it comes. So ask God to build you up so that you can better handle times of crises in your life.

*Cry out, "Lord, I need You!"* When you are starving, no one cares if you stuff yourself or break the rules of etiquette. Compassionate people are glad to see a starving person eat. So dig in!

*Go from hunger prayer to another expression of prayer.* It's okay to dig in when you're starving, but it's a different matter when you eat a normal meal with normal people. It's offensive to them when you chew with your mouth open. So remember, there's a proper time for prayers of desperation, just as there's a time proper time for other types of prayers.

*Commit to praying at scheduled times.* The key to leading a balanced Christian life is to keep your hunger in balance. Eating at proper times will keep your hunger in control, and praying at proper times will keep your spiritual hunger for God in line. Just as you stay healthy by eating the proper food at regular intervals, a well-balanced prayer life will help you grow in Christ.

# when we need to prevail

*Remember, it is sin to know what you ought to do and then not do it.*
JAMES 4:17, *NLT*

A man was sleeping soundly in his bed when a neighbor friend knocked on his door. The friend asked the man for some bread, but since it was midnight and the man was tired, he responded, "Do not trouble me. The door is locked and my family is in bed. I'm not going to get up to give it you right now!" But the man's friend kept pounding and pounding on the door. Finally, the man realized that he would not get any sleep that night if he did not comply with his friend's wishes, so he rolled out of bed and gave his friend as many loaves as he needed to make him go away.

Jesus told this parable in Luke 11:598, concluding with the following note about the man in the story:

> Though he will not rise and give to him because he is his friend, yet because of his *persistence* he will rise and give him as many as he needs. So I say to you, ask, and it will be given to you; seek, and you will find; knock, and it will be opened to you (vv. 8-9, emphasis added).

Jesus honors *persistent* prayer. We sometimes need to keep praying regardless of fatigue, obstacles in our path or discouragement. When we say prevailing prayers, we enter into God's presence with a will of steel and determine to never quit, no matter what. Wesley L. Duwel, in his book *Prevailing Prayer,* provides an excellent definition of prevailing in prayer:

> To prevail is to be successful in the face of difficulty, to completely dominate, to overcome and tie up. Prevailing prayer is prayer that pushes right through all difficulties and obstacles, drives back all the opposing forces of Satan, and secures the will of God. Its purpose is to accomplish God's will on earth. Prevailing prayer not only takes the initiative, but continues on the offence for God until spiritual victory is won.[1]

In this chapter, we will examine prevailing in prayer for ourselves and for others who are in need of God's power in their lives.

## THE PURPOSE OF PREVAILING IN PRAYER

Why must we prevail in prayer? One reason is that our flesh is weak and we need to stay focused on what God has commanded us to do. When Jesus was in the Garden of Gethsemane the night before He was crucified, He asked the disciples to sit and keep watch with Him as He prayed. But when He returned to where the disciples were, He discovered that they had all fallen asleep. "What, could you not watch with Me one hour?" Jesus asked. "Watch and pray, lest you enter into temptation. The spirit indeed is willing, but the flesh is weak" (Matt. 26:40-41).

Another reason why we must prevail in prayer is that there are times when God will test our sincerity. In Psalm 17:3, David expressed this idea when he said to the Lord, "You have tested my heart; You have visited me in the night; You have tried me and have found nothing; I have purposed that my mouth shall not transgress." Job understood that the trials that he was enduring served as a test of his character: "But He knows the way that I take; when He has tested me, I shall come forth as gold" (Job 23:10). And James realized that the trials and persecutions that Early Christians were experiencing would strengthen their faith:

> Dear brothers and sisters, whenever trouble comes your way, let it be an opportunity for joy. For when your faith is tested, your endurance has a chance to grow. So let it grow, for when your endurance is fully developed, you will be strong in character and ready for anything. God blesses the people who patiently endure testing (Jas. 1:2-4,12, *NLT*).

God may not immediately answer all of our prayers, for if He always gave us quick answers to our requests, we would be encouraged to pray superficially. Instead, God tests us to determine our resolve.

In the Old Testament, God tested Jacob's resolve when He wrestled with Jacob until the morning light: "Now when He saw that He did not prevail against him, He touched the socket of his hip; and the socket of Jacob's hip was out of joint as He wrested with him" (Gen. 32:25). Yet despite the pain that he undoubtedly was experiencing, Jacob refused to let go until he received a blessing from the Lord. So the Lord said, "Your name shall no longer be called Jacob, but Israel; for you have struggled with God and with men, and have prevailed" (v. 28).

We should also prevail in prayer because we're in warfare for the souls of others. The Christian life is not a tea party; it's a battlefield. Paul said, "We do not wrestle against flesh and blood, but against principalities, against powers, against the rulers of the darkness of this age, against spiritual hosts of wickedness in the heavenly places" (Eph. 6:12). We must take the pledge of the intercessor:

I will put my whole heart in prayer, and press forward,
I will give all my energy until I have none left,
I will not leave any petition unprayed,
And I will stay in God's presence until I am victorious.

One way that we can prevail for others is by committing to spend our time and energy in prayer for them until they experience salvation in Christ.

## REDEMPTIVE PRAYER

The word "redemption" means paying a price or buying back. When we say redemptive prayers for others, we pay the price in intercession so that lost people are redeemed. This doesn't necessarily mean that other people's salvation is based on our prayers. But it does mean that we continue to give our time and energy in prayer until they exhibit evidences of having experienced salvation.

This is not to say that it is our suffering and prayers that redeem others. Some people wrongly interpret Paul's words to the Colossians, "I now rejoice in my sufferings for you, and fill up in my flesh what is lacking in the afflictions of Christ, for the sake of His body, which is the church" (Col. 1:24) to mean that it was Paul's sufferings that helped others come to Christ. What Paul was really saying in this verse was that while preaching the gospel, he endured great suffering—he was beaten, thrown in prison, robbed and stoned by a crowd; he also suffered from natural calamities such as a shipwreck and storms. Paul suffered through these things and persevered in preaching the gospel. Eventually, the Colossians were saved.

Paul understood that only the blood of Christ could redeem those who were lost in sin. When Adam and Eve sinned in the

Garden of Eden, all of humankind received a sin nature that was bent toward the world and the flesh. But Christ came into this world to pay the price of redemption, not with "corruptible things, like silver or gold . . . but with the precious blood of Christ, as of a lamb" (1 Pet. 1:18-19). The price of redemption can *only be paid through the blood of Jesus Christ*. Redemptive prayer means continually pleading the blood of Christ until those who are lost come into the kingdom of God.

Redemptive prayer involves a sacrifice on our part. When the Israelites sinned against God by worshiping a golden calf, Moses went before the Lord and offered himself as a sacrifice so that the people might be saved. "Oh, these people have committed a great sin," Moses cried to the Lord, "and have made for themselves a god of gold! Yet now, if You will forgive their sin—but if not, I pray, blot me out of Your book which You have written'" (Exod. 32:31-32).

How intently did Moses pray? Notice the dash in the above passage. What does this dash mean? Possibly it means that Moses came to the end of himself. He did not know what else to say to the Lord—he stood speechless before God. His redemptive prayer went beyond words to the very yearning of his heart.

Paul expressed the same sentiment when he offered to give himself up so that the people of Israel could be saved. In Romans 9:3, Paul wrote, "For I could wish that I myself were accursed from Christ for my brethren, my countrymen." The word "accurse" in this verse is synonymous with asking to be cast into hell!

Redemptive praying means identifying ourselves with the ones for whom we are praying, just as Jesus identified Himself with the transgressors (see Isa. 53:5-7). It means agonizing over sin, just as Jesus agonized for our sins in the Garden of Gethsemane. We need to realize that we *can* influence God through our prayers and that our intercession can lead others to salvation.

## THE PRICE OF REDEMPTIVE PRAYER

Praying for other people in this manner is extremely difficult, for when we truly say redemptive prayers, the sin of those for whom we pray will break our hearts. We will agonize over the fact that our loved ones have turned their backs on the love of Christ. We will agonize over their open transgression and disobedience. When we intercede for people on this level, we will voluntarily take on the grief and pain caused by their rebellious attitudes.

True redemptive intercession is a struggle, and it's exhausting. It's a lot like a wrestling match, in which one person tries to pin the other to the floor. In fact, Paul uses this same metaphor in Ephesians 6:12. Contestants use every bit of energy and mental sharpness when wrestling, and we must do the same in redemptive prayer. We wrestle against Satan for the release of those whom he is holding captive in sin. We wrestle against evil principalities and addictive sin in the one for whom we pray. The more grievous the sin, the harder we must wrestle. The longer the person has been in sin, the longer we must wrestle. The more that sin has held that person in bondage, the more we must agonize in prayer. We strive against the wrath of God that has been poured out against transgression.

Redemptive prayer also involves forgiveness. As Jesus hung on the cross, he prayed for his accusers, saying, "Father, forgive them, for they do not know what they do" (Luke 23:34). In the book of Acts, when a crowd took Stephen out of the city of Jerusalem in order to stone him, Stephen knelt down and cried with a loud voice, "Lord, do not charge them with this sin" (Acts 7:60). Jesus and Stephen forgave their executioners. In the same way, we must forgive those for whom we intervene.

Daniel prayed—*agonized*—for 21 days without an answer. "In those days," he wrote, "I, Daniel, was mourning three full weeks. I ate no pleasant food, no meat or wine came into my mouth"

(Dan. 10:2-3). After three weeks had passed, Daniel encountered an angel of the Lord, who said:

> Do not fear, Daniel, for from the first day that you set your heart to understand, and to humble yourself before your God, your words were heard; and I have come because of your words. But the prince of the kingdom of Persia [a demon] withstood me twenty-one days (Dan. 10:12-13).

Daniel didn't fully understand why his prayers had not been answered, but he prevailed in prayer until the answer came. In the same way, Satan will try to oppose our efforts when we pray. We need to be persistent in our prayers for ourselves and others and prevail against our weariness until the answer comes.

# Your Assignment

*Determine to spend time in intercession.* Daniel prayed three times a day (see Dan. 6:10). On one occasion, he prayed and fasted for 21 days (see Dan. 10:3). If you intend to prevail in prayer, set aside a long period of time to pray and then pray continually for your request. You haven't prevailed until you have spent uninterrupted time in prayer.

*Build up a prayer reservoir of habit, attitude and passion.* This does not mean that you can build up a package of "good deeds" in heaven that will carry you through rough times, but that you have developed a commitment to always pray in the face of a great need. Each time you attempt to prevail in prayer, you tap into that reservoir of commitment.

*Pray with your whole being.* Pray with your intellect as you remember what God has promised to you in His Word. Pray with your emotion as you pour your tears out to God and plead for your request. Pray with your will as you determine to prevail and never give up.

*Review your prayer list to determine for whom you will say prayers of redemption.* Not everyone will qualify for redemptive prayer, for you will have a burden on your heart for some people but not for others. Make a list of those for whom you know you should intercede. (This may include unsaved relatives, friends who suffer from addiction, and others with severe problems in their lives.)

*Ask God to increase the burden.* Redemptive prayer will go beyond your normal prayer time, so ask God for a heavier burden for targeted individuals. When God answers with a greater burden or deeper zeal, you know He is leading you to redemptive prayer. Also ask God for faith to move the mountain in that person's life.

*Let your intensity drive you.* Prevailing in prayer is something God initially gives you, and you then resolve to never give up. Make a vow to prevail in prayer—for yourself or for those whom over you pray redemptive prayers—until the answer comes.

**Note**

1. Wesley L. Duwel, *Prevailing Prayer* (Grand Rapids, MI: Zondervan: 1990), n.p.

CHAPTER FOURTEEN

# when we see injustice

*Learn to do good; seek justice, reprove the oppressor;*
*defend the fatherless, plead for the widow.*

ISAIAH 1:17

There is much injustice in the world today. Warlords in developing nations terrorize the populace, deprive people of food, and commit acts of genocide. Multinational industries pollute the environment and enslave their workers to inadequate wages and tyrannical work conditions. Corporate executives bilk their companies out of millions of dollars. Politicians take bribes. Innocent people are thrown into prison.

What is the role of the Christian in the face of so much injustice? Many speak out against injustice but have no idea how to confront it. Some shrug their shoulders and just say, "What can I do?" A few do one good deed and hope that their contribution makes a difference in the world.

It's like the two men who were walking down the beach and saw thousands of dying clams that had been washed up on shore. The first man picked up a single clam and threw it back in the sea. "You can't save all the clams," the second man remarked. "True," said the first man, "but I can save at least one." But is saving just *one* all that a Christian can do?

## PASSIVE RESISTANCE

In August 1960, when Martin Luther King, Jr., and 75 students entered a department store in Atlanta, Georgia, and requested service at a whites-only lunch counter, King and 36 of the students were arrested. Three years later, Alabama Circuit Judge W. A. Jenkins issued an order prohibiting King from taking part in sit-ins, picketing or other demonstrations in the city of Birmingham, Alabama. But King defied the order, and as a result he was arrested and placed in solitary confinement.

After King was arrested, the local white Christian clergy took out a full-page advertisement in the *Birmingham News,* labeling King a troublemaker. When King read the advertisement, he drafted a defense of his actions in the margin of the newspaper and on scraps of toilet paper and chronicled his view of passive resistance to racism in America. King's notes were later published in *Letters from the Birmingham Jail.*[1]

Perhaps one of the 10 greatest sermons in the history of Christianity was King's "I Have a Dream" sermon, delivered from the steps of the Lincoln Memorial in Washington, D.C., in August 1963:

> I have a dream that one day the state of Alabama, whose governor's lips are presently dripping with the words of interposition and nullification, will be transformed into a situation where little black boys and girls will be able to join hands with little white boys and white girls and walk together as sisters and brothers.

King's "I Have a Dream" sermon changed the way the nation viewed equality and eventually led to the civil rights legislation in Congress. The civil rights legislation established equal rights for Black Americans under the law and affected all Americans in many ways—from installing special curbs for people in wheelchairs to banning stores from segregating their bathrooms and drinking fountains.

King's civil rights movement was rooted in the belief that all humans are made in the image of God: "So God created man in His own image; in the image of God He created him; male and female He created them" (Gen. 1:27). King believed that all people—male or female, young or old, rich or poor, healthy or sick—deserved to be treated with respect and equality under the law. Like the prophet Amos (who King quoted in his "I Have a Dream" sermon), King desired for "justice [to] run down like water, and righteousness like a mighty stream" (Amos 5:24).

King formed his policy of passive resistance based on the writings and experience of Mahatma Gandhi, who in the 1930s organized people in India to aggressively—but nonviolently—revolt against the British government. Ghandi resisted British rule by having his followers boycott British-produced salt, tea and cloth. He set an example by weaving his own cloth and urging millions of others to do the same. Gandhi led marches and suffered for his cause. Martin Luther King, Jr., and Gandhi were men who saw injustice in the world and decided to make a stand against that injustice.

## THE WEAPON OF PRAYER

Jesus was also born into a world in which an authoritarian and oppressive government forced its will on the people. The Jews of Palestine were people under occupation by the powerful Roman army. They had a limited sphere of freedom, and the desire of many Israelites was to drive the hated Romans from their land into the sea.

A small band of rebels, called "zealots," fought hit-and-run battles against the Romans—with little, if any, results. When people recognized Jesus as the promised Messiah, they seized on passages in the Old Testament that speak of the Messiah coming as a "conquering king" and assumed that Christ would be a great military leader. Many probably thought that the Messiah would join with the zealots to rid Palestine of the Romans. When Jesus performed miracles such as feeding 5,000 people with 2 small fish and 5 barley loaves, the people wanted to make Him king. But this was not what Jesus wanted. Christ had not come to rule the people by force but to conquer them with love and rule their hearts.

This was Jesus' greatest opportunity to take up arms and physically revolt against injustice. But He chose not to do it. Instead, He sent His disciples in a small boat to the other side of the Sea of Galilee and then left the revolt-hungry crowd behind to seek out a place to pray: "When He had sent the multitudes away, He went up on the mountain by Himself to pray. Now when evening came, He was alone there" (Matt. 14:23).

As Christians, should we stand against the injustice we see in this world? Absolutely. As 1 Peter 3:17-18 states, "It is better, if it is the will of God, to suffer for doing good . . . for Christ also suffered once for sins, the just for the unjust, that He might bring us to God." But we should not forget that our primary weapon against mass injustice is *prayer*. Prayer is a peaceful weapon that can solve the problems of this intolerant world. Our prayers can purposefully intercede against evil, change the course of this world, and right the wrongs therein.

## PREVAILING AGAINST INJUSTICE

When we truly believe that prayer makes a difference and pray against the injustices of the world, we become the voice of the voiceless and the power of the powerless as we connect with the God of heaven and intercede for those who need help. We ask God to bring light into a dark world and pray for righteousness to destroy wickedness.

We should always begin our battle against injustice by recognizing that we are wrestling against the spiritual forces of darkness in this world (see Eph. 6:12). We do not pray against the actual *people* who deliver evil in this world—the pimp, the corrupt politician, the drug pusher—but focus our prayers against the *evil* that causes the injustice in our world. The battle is much deeper than mere individuals; it goes to the core of evil in the world.

In Matthew 16:18, Jesus told Peter, "Upon this rock I will build my church; and the gates of hell shall not prevail against it" (*KJV*). Hell is desperately trying to keep righteousness out of its gates. But the Church is prevailing against the gates of hell and is opposing Satan's power to corrupt people and destroy lives. Jesus said that we should continue to pray for the kingdom of God to come to this world and to deliver us from the evil one (see Matt. 6:10,13).

Jesus overcame the power of death and hell through His resurrection. He has demonstrated His authority over spiritual evil and is now seated at the right hand of the Father, "far above all principality and power and might and dominion . . . And He put all things under His feet" (Eph. 1:21-22). Jesus has the power to deliver us from the evil one, for "all authority has been given to [Him] in heaven and on earth" (Matt. 28:18). We can call upon His power in heaven to prevail against the evil in this world.

So what should Christians do when they see crime, racism, sexism, nationalism and corruption in this world? We should truly believe that Christians can make a difference in this world and prevail in prayer against the injustice that we encounter every day.

# YOUR ASSIGNMENT

*Pray for the positive ministry of preaching the gospel and planting new churches.* Don't make the primary focus of your prayers a negative campaign against abortion, crime-infested neighborhoods, or the gambling industry. Yes, do pray against those evils, but also remember to pray in a positive manner for people to experience the salvation of Christ.

*Wage spiritual warfare against the enemy.* Paul describes the armor that you must wear to wage spiritual warfare against the enemy: "Gird your waist with truth, put on the breastplate of righteousness, shod your feet with the gospel; take up the shield of faith, the helmet of salvation and the sword of the Spirit, which is the Word of God" (Eph. 6:14-17, *ELT*). Paul then gives us the key to battle: "Praying always with all prayer and supplication in the Spirit" (v. 18). Warfare prayer is wrestling with evil, because evil is always present.

*Make a list of evil and pray against it.* There is so much evil in this world that no one can mention every possible source, but try to list a few sources of evil for which you feel especially burdened. Let the Holy Spirit lead you, and then pray against the evil that you have listed.

*Pray for the enlightening of the Holy Spirit.* Pray that people may see their transgressions and become convicted of sin, righteousness and judgment (see John 16:8-11). Paul states, "The god of this age has blinded [the minds of those] who do not believe" (2 Cor. 4:4). People who are blinded to God will be cruel, unjust and take evil to a deeper level.

*Claim the blood of Jesus Christ.* The key to spiritual victory is to overcome evil through the blood of the Lamb (see Rev. 12:11). When you plead the blood of the Lamb, you are protected from the evil one and you receive power to conquer evil. Perhaps the old hymn describes it best:

"There's power in the blood of the Lamb!"[2]

*Claim ultimate victory by praying daily, "Your kingdom come."* Because you have spiritual weapons to fight the war against evil and injustice, you can conquer through the blood of Jesus Christ. You may lose battles along the way, but you'll win the final victory. You *can* make a difference in the world by praying for God to transform the hearts and minds of individuals.

*Exercise authority against the evil one.* We have no authority in ourselves, but in the Word of God there is power to change lives . . . to heal the sick . . . to break curses . . . and to cast out demons. For more information on casting out demons, see Doris M. Wagner, *How to Minister Freedom* (Ventura, CA: Regal Books, 2005), and John L. Nevius and F. F. Ellinwood, *Demon Possession and Allied Themes* (Grand Rapids, MI: Kregel Publications, 1968 reprint edition).

*Deal with your fears.* What scares you? Perhaps you are afraid of the gambling industry, or terrorists, or drugs, or some other giant. Perhaps you are afraid of what the demons might do to you if you took a stand against them. But John assures us, "He who is in you is greater than he who is in the world" (1 John 4:4). So pray with boldness against the enemy and trust in the power of God to protect you from the enemy. As the writer of Hebrews states, "So we may boldly say: 'The LORD is my helper; I will not fear. What can man do to me?'" (Heb. 13:6).

**Notes**
1. Martin Luther King, Jr., *Letters from the Birmingham Jail* (San Francisco, CA: HarperCollins, 1994).
2. Lewis E. Jones, "There is Power in the Blood," written at a camp meeting at Mountain Lake Park, Maryland in 1899. http://members.tripod.com/~Synergy_2/lyrics/power.html (accessed November 22, 2004).

# when we recognize the sins of others

*I pray before You now . . . and confess the sins of the children of Israel that we have sinned against You. Both my fathers and I have sinned.*
NEHEMIAH 1:6, *ELT*

November 1995 marked the nine-hundredth anniversary of Pope Urban II's proclamation for Christians in Europe to take up arms and liberate the Holy Land from Muslim occupation—a proclamation that would lead to numerous atrocities and injustices committed in the name of Christ against the Arab and Jewish worlds. To mark the anniversary of this proclamation, a group of Christians decided to band together and establish "The Reconciliation Walk."

Starting from the city of Cologne, Germany (and other cities in Europe), members of the prayer journey traveled along the route of the Crusaders and met with various city officials (primarily Muslim and Jewish) to confess the sins of their ancestors and ask for forgiveness. Along the route, members handed out a statement of apology to explain the purpose of their journey:

> Nine hundred years ago, our forefathers carried the name of Jesus Christ in battle across the Middle East. Fueled by fear, greed and hatred, they betrayed the name of Christ by conducting themselves in a manner contrary to His wishes and character. The Crusaders lifted the banner of

the Cross above your people. By this act they corrupted its true meaning of reconciliation, forgiveness and selfless love. . . . Where they were motivated by hatred and prejudice, we offer love and brotherhood. Jesus the Messiah came to give life. Forgive us for allowing His name to be associated with death.[1]

Similar prayer journeys have occurred in recent years for other atrocities committed in the past. In May 2002, a team of 20 people from 11 nations traveled along a former slave-trade route in France, wearing replicas of the yokes and chains used by slave traders in that nation. As the team journeyed to the former slave-trade ports of Rouen, Honfleur, St. Malo, Nantes, La Rochelle and Bordeaux, they handed out leaflets apologizing for the role that Christians played in the great injustice of the slave trade. Many descendants of former slaves living in France were deeply moved by the actions of this group of people—"at last!" was the most common reaction.[2]

The purpose of each of these prayer journeys was for members to practice something known as *identificational repentance*. Similar to redemptive prayers, prayers of identificational repentance involve dealing with the unrepented transgressions of others (including the sins of past generations) and accepting the consequences of that sin. In this chapter, we will discuss this topic in detail and examine how this concept relates in the context of Scripture.

## JUSTICE AND MERCY

Identificational repentance involves the prayers of our troubled spirits when we are deeply concerned about the sins of others. When we encounter abortion, homosexuality or any other type of injustice, we enter the fray of battle to pray over the fallout of that sin upon our society or upon the Church. However, instead of praying for God's judgment on those who have sinned, we ask God to forgive the transgressors' sins. John Dawson, in his powerful book *Healing America's Wounds*, sums up the idea well: "Identificational repentance is a new way of helping the downtrodden, giving liberty to the oppressed, and placating the imminent judgment of God."[3]

This is not to say that through our prayers we obtain forgiveness for individuals who have sinned through. In Luke 13:3, Jesus said, "But unless you repent you will all likewise perish." People must repent for themselves to obtain God's forgiveness. However, the focus of identificational repentance is not on forgiving the person who committed the sin but on dealing with the *consequences of God's pending judgment* against that sin. When we identify with a past or present sin of other people and repent of that sin, we are in effect asking God to hold back the punishment that is due.

When we pray identificational repentance, we champion the rights of those who have been sinned against and ask for the spiritual release of those who are sinning. We look at the world's sins through the eyes of mercy and forgiveness and ask for God's *mercy* instead of His *justice*. Justice cuts two ways: It punishes the sinner, but it also punishes Christians and the Church because we live in a world in which sin was committed and in which the fallout of its consequences can be felt. Mercy also has two edges: It allows us to experience the grace of God and receive the outpouring of God's blessings, but it also extends to unsaved people and the culture. God's mercy and blessings extend to society through the Christians who live there.

One of the greatest things about identificational repentance is that it enables us to remove the gall of bitterness that may afflict our souls when we see injustice in the world. The thought of babies being aborted can certainly make us become extremely bitter and reactionary to anyone who has an abortion, but we can release that bitterness by confessing the sins that are done in the abortion clinics.

God's love is a better way. Through prayer, we can love people into the Kingdom. Remember, some of those individuals who we may have wanted God to punish have later found Christ and are now serving God with us. If God had punished these people every time they sinned, they would never have experienced His mercy. And what if God had punished us for all the sins we committed before we accepted His salvation?

## Identificational Repentance in Scripture

Is identificational repentance biblical? Many people believe that the concept has no biblical basis and cannot be supported by examples from Scripture. However, listen to the words of Daniel:

> And I prayed to the LORD my God, and made confession, and said, "O Lord, great and awesome God . . . we have sinned and committed iniquity, we have done wickedly and rebelled, even by departing from Your precepts and Your judgments. . . . to us belongs shame of face, to our kings, our princes, and our fathers, because we have sinned against You" (Dan. 9:4-5,8).

Daniel was on his face before God confessing his sin, but he was not confessing *his* sin only. Seventy years after Israel was taken captive, Daniel was suffering the sins of his forefathers and was motivated to deal with those sins. Daniel identified with the sins of his ancestors and did not exclude himself from those transgressions—for he knew that if he had lived back then, he might have committed the same sins. Daniel repented on behalf of the people of Israel and became a mediator between them and God. He confessed the sins that put the nation into captivity so that the consequences of those sins could be dealt and the Israelites could return home. Daniel based his prayer of identificational repentance on the grace of God, saying, "We do not present our supplications before You because of our righteous deeds, but because of Your great mercies" (Dan. 9:18). Daniel pleaded God's mercy!

Identificational repentance was not an event limited only to Daniel. When Nehemiah prayed, he identified with the sins of those who put him into captivity:

> Please let Your ear be attentive and Your eyes open, that You may hear the prayer of Your servant which I pray before You now . . . and confess the sins of the children of Israel which we have sinned against You. Both my father's house and I have sinned (Neh. 1:6).

Notice that Nehemiah included himself in his prayer of identificational repentance when he wrote, "Both *my father's house and I* have sinned." And Moses also entered into identificational repentance when he interceded for Israel after they sinned against God by making the golden calf (see Exod. 32:31-32).

## PRAYING PATIENTLY AND CONTINUALLY

Will our identificational repentance on behalf of others somehow make it easier for them to become saved? Perhaps! Our act will give them another day to live before God, and as long as a person lives, he or she has an opportunity to repent and turn to God.

Remember, when we enter into identificational repentance, not everything will be instantly transformed. Although we enter the infinite mercy of God when we come into His presence, we also struggle against the powers of sin. All sin—whether we are dealing with racism, abortion, sexual perversion, or whatever—are very powerful and pervasive. Sin has captured the hearts and desires of people everywhere, so it's going to take a tremendous amount of prayer to turn around any situation.

Even Jesus' sacrifice on Calvary didn't produce instantaneous results in the hearts of every person for whom Christ died. Many people hardened their hearts toward the death of Christ and persecuted the disciples (see Acts 4:1-21). Some Christians, such as Ananias and Sapphira, sinned volitionally against the blood of Christ (see Acts 5:1-11). Just as the sacrifice of Jesus didn't immediately change the heart of every person after His death and resurrection, so our redemptive prayers will not instantaneously change the situation. We must *prevail* in prayer—praying patiently and continually.

# YOUR ASSIGNMENT

*Make a list of those sins that you feel threaten society the most.* This list should include those things that will bring God's punishment on society.

*Practice identificational repentance.* Remember, identificational repentance involves the prayers of your troubled spirit when you are deeply concerned about the sins others. Begin your prayer of identificational repentance by confessing the sins of others so that God will forgive them and withhold His judgment on our society.

*Pray for those who are involved in sin.* Once you have confessed the sins of others, pray for those specific individuals involved in this sin. Intercede on their behalf so that they may come to Christ. "The Lord . . . is longsuffering toward us, not willing that any should perish but that all should come to repentance" (2 Pet. 3:9).

*Let go of any bitterness.* Release any pain and bitterness that the sins of others may have caused you by confessing those sins. Ask God to help you love those people into His kingdom instead of persecuting and seeking justice against them.

*Confess your own sins.* When you enter identificational repentance and God holds back His punishment, you win. When you deal with your own sin and Gods pours out His mercy upon you, you win. The mercy of God must always win out over the justice of God. And in the end, God is glorified.

## Notes

1. B. A. Robinson, "Christian Apology for the Crusades: The Reconciliation Walk," Ontario Consultants on Religious Tolerance. http://www.religious tolerance.org/chr_cru1.htm (accessed January 9, 2006).
2. "Ambassadors in Chains—France 2002," The Lifeline Expedition. http://www. reconcile.org/index.html (accessed January 9, 2006).
3. John Dawson, *Healing America's Wounds* (Ventura, CA: Regal Books, 1995), n.p.

# when we need healing

*And the prayer of faith will save the sick, and the Lord will raise him up.*
*And if he has committed sins, he will be forgiven.*

JAMES 5:15

I was a 20-year-old Bible College student pastoring at Westminster Presbyterian Church in Savannah, Georgia, on the weekends when I received a call from Mrs. Van Brackle after 11 o'clock at night. Mrs. Van Brackle, a lady in her 80s, suffered from cataracts and asked me to come to her home to pray for her. It was quite an imposition, but I decided to go and see her anyway.

Arriving past midnight, I walked into Mrs. Van Brackle's room and found her two young grandsons waiting for me. They had been drinking beer all evening and were now half soused. Earlier in the day, they had taken their grandmother to a city over 100 miles away to see a famous faith healer who was holding a meeting in a large tent. Apparently, the faith healer had been unable to heal Mrs. Van Brackle and had said that the cause of this failure was because Mrs. Van Brackle lacked faith. I think Mrs. Van Brackle and her two grandsons wondered if I had the faith to heal her. I felt on the spot.

Right before I prayed, Mrs. Van Brackle asked if I would lay hands on her eyes as I prayed. I had never done that before—or even seen it done before—so I wasn't sure how to respond. But I did know that the Bible taught that Jesus laid His hands on people, so I hesitated briefly and then reached out, placed my hands on Mrs. Van Brackle, and asked God to heal her cataracts and give her sight.

After I left the home, I forgot about the situation until I returned for my next weekend ministry. Mrs. Van Brackle sent for me again, and when I walked into her room, she asked for my Bible. Opening it, she began reading a passage in Isaiah. I didn't get what she was doing at first, but then she said, "I can see to read—you healed me!"

Her pronouncement about *me* healing her made me very uncomfortable. I always struggle with whether I am doing something for Christ or for my own self-glory, and the whole "laying on of hands" thing seemed Pentecostal to me—I didn't want people to think that I was Pentecostal! As a result, I didn't tell anyone about the healing that next day in church. In fact, I didn't tell anyone for over 30 years.

So what did I miss? I could have strengthened Mrs. Van Brackle's family by giving God the glory for what He had done. I could have strengthened the church by telling them that God still does miracles. I could have strengthened my own faith and believed more in the power of God. But at this time in my life, the idea that I could pray for healing and people would *actually* be healed made me uneasy.

Why is this so often the case? Why is it difficult for us to believe that our prayers can actually bring healing? Why doesn't healing always occur? In this chapter, we will examine some of these issues.

## THE GIFT OF HEALING AND THE PRAYER OF HEALING

In 1 Corinthians 12:30, Paul asks the question, "Do all have gifts of healing?" Obviously, Paul is implying that not all of us have this gift. So, the first thing to understand about healing is that there is a difference between the *gift of healing* and the *prayer of healing*.

In the book of Acts, we see that some people were healed through the gift of healing. Some of the apostles possessed this gift: "the apostles [performed] many miraculous signs and wonders among the people" (Acts 5:12, *NLT*). The book of Acts also states that "crowds came in from the villages around Jerusalem, bringing their sick and those possessed by evil spirits, and they were all healed" (v. 16, *NLT*).

Some people say that the gift of healing is one of those spiritual gifts that were evident only during the time of the apostles and that when the apostles passed off the scene, so did this particular gift of healing. Saint Augustine, for instance, believed that the gift of healing had passed out of existence.[1] However, when a person in his church was healed of epileptic fits, Augustine changed his opinion and added a new section on healing in his book, *The City of God*.[2] Actually, this might be too strong a description of Augustine's reversal—a careful reading of his works seems to suggest that he still believed the gift of healing had ceased, but that *prayer for healing* was valid. I tend to agree with Augustine that God still heals, but that He does it in answer to prayer.

Praying for healing should be as normal to us as teaching Sunday School or visiting the needy. Of course, this is not to say that we should go overboard on healing. Some churches have so magnified healing that they are known for their "healing lines." Some individuals, calling themselves "faith healers," have mistakenly believed that they have the power to heal, when in fact the healing came in answer to prayer. What I am saying here is that healing should not be overemphasized, nor should it be underemphasized. We need to keep healing in the proper perspective.

When we refuse to believe in physical healing, we denigrate the physical body to a place of second importance. We basically say that God saves our souls but does nothing for our bodies. We make the soul the only shrine of spirituality, which is a false dichotomy because we cannot have the presence of God in our spiritual temple and not let His glory shine through our bodies. God cares as much about our physical lives as He does about our spiritual lives. He cares about what we eat, how we discipline our body, what clothes we put on, and whether we are suffering.

Because God saved us, our souls will live forever—but so will our bodies. In the resurrection, our bodies will join with our souls and we will live forever. This means that salvation affects our whole life—our body and our souls. Shouldn't we then expect healing in our emotions and mind as well as in our body and soul?

## HOW HEALING COMES TO US

Before we look at the role of prayer to reverse sickness, let's examine how our bodies and souls get healthy. God uses many different ways to make us healthy. For instance, God gives us medical doctors who do a variety of things to keep us healthy—they cut away cancer; give us antibiotics to fight disease; advise us about our appetite, rest, recreation and physical exercise. The Bible teaches that "every good gift and every perfect gift is from above" (Jas. 1:17), which suggests that the gift of medicine is from God. (Of course, it is important to remember that for all that a doctor does, he or she does not make us healthy. Doctors may remove the cause of the disease, but in the final analysis, it is the body that heals itself.)

But there is another gift—the gift of counseling through ministers and other godly therapists. God gives us psychologists, psychiatrists, and those who are able to deal with mental pathology (whether it be neuroses, psychoses, or simply a mentally-disturbing problem). These therapists help people think in healthy patterns and aid in the healing process for people's emotions and minds. In the long run, patients become holistically healthy.

God also gives us a vast army of other specialists from the other branches of medicine. Each of these specialists deals with a very specific part of our physical bodies or our minds. God has given each of these individuals to us so that we might have complete mental and physical health.

To these we should add the power of healing prayer. Sometimes God heals directly by His power alone, but at other times He heals through prayer and the use of medicine, surgery, exercise, drugs, or other forms of therapy. And how do we pray for healing? We pray for God to give wisdom to the therapists to diagnose our problem and wisdom for the doctors to prescribe the proper medicine. We pray for God to effectively use drugs or medicine for its intended cure in our body. And we pray for God to stop anything that would be detrimental to our health.

We should also pray for God to reveal any unknown or unseen factors that bring about our illnesses. In the late 1960s, I had a teaching colleague at Trinity Evangelical Divinity School who became severely ill and was admitted to a hospital. The hospital ran various tests to try to determine why my colleague had become sick, but they were unable to uncover the cause of his illness. However, after a short stay at the hospital, my colleague's condition quickly improved. He was released and returned to his home.

Once he was home again, my colleague's illness returned once again. He returned to the hospital, but the doctors were still unable to find the source of the problem. However, they did observe that he appeared to be suffering from the same symptoms that inner city children who were exposed to lead poisoning suffered from at the time. But my colleague was a suburbanite and had not been exposed to lead paint (or so he thought). So the doctors continued their search for another cause of the problem.

Then my colleague's entire family came down with the same symptoms. At that point, they stopped praying just for healing and began praying for God to help them find the unseen causes of their physical problem. Shortly thereafter, they discovered that the culprit was a set of beautiful china cups that they had bought on a mission tour. The cups had not been thoroughly fired in a kiln to seal the ceramic finish, and when the family added hot tea, the tea melted the lead paint in the cups. God answered my colleague's prayer for healing by answering a prayer for illumination as to what was causing his family's illness.

In the end, we can go to two extremes praying for healing: (1) relying only on prayer and refusing any medical diagnosis or any drugs; or (2) relying exclusively on doctors and therapists and turning to prayer only as a last resort when the prescribed medicines and therapies fail. Should we not seek healing from both the medical field and prayer at the same time?

## HAVING FAITH IN GOD'S HEALING POWER

Prayers for healing should always begin with the soul of the sick person. When Jesus healed people, the majority of the time he focused first on the spiritual life of the sick person. For example, Jesus told the man who had not walked for 38 years to "sin no more, lest a worse thing come upon you" (John 5:14). On other occasions, Jesus told the healed person to go tell about his healing to the priests. Jesus always pointed the healed person toward God.

However, when we pray for the spiritual condition of the sick person, we need to make sure that we don't let that become a copout for our lack of faith that God can also *physically* heal the person. Most of us have no trouble believing that God can change a person's thinking, but when it comes to believing that the person can actually receive physical healing—well, that takes a great deal more faith.

This is especially true when the person's physical problems are severe. When the cancer is advanced, it's hard to pray for healing. When someone is severely crippled, it's hard to believe that God can make him or her walk again. So when we pray for healing, we should begin with our own lack of faith. We have to pray like the father of the epileptic demon-possessed boy: "Lord, I believe; help my unbelief!" (Mark 9:24). We must have faith for healing before we can pray for physical healing.

At the beginning of this chapter, I recounted the story of how God brought healing to Mrs. Van Brackle when I laid hands on her and prayed over her. As I mentioned, my lack of faith in this instance kept me from trusting that God could do bigger things in Mrs. Van Brackle's family than just heal her eyes. In the end, due to my lack of faith, I missed out on strengthening Mrs. Van Brackle's family, the church, and my own life. We need to have faith in God's power so that we don't limit the work that He wants to do in each of our lives.

Now, this is not to say that everyone for whom we pray in faith will be healed. After all, even Jesus didn't heal everyone who came to Him. For instance, when Jesus traveled to Jerusalem and approached a place known as the Pool of Bethesda, He saw "a great multitude of sick people, blind, lame, paralyzed, waiting for the moving of the water" (John 5:3). However, Jesus healed only the man who had been lame for 38 years (see vv. 5-9).

On other occasions, Jesus cured everyone who came to Him for healing (see Matt. 12:15). And sometimes the Bible says that Jesus healed *many* of those who were ill, but not *all*: "At evening, when the sun had set, they brought to Him *all* who were sick . . . [and] He healed *many* who were sick with various diseases" (Mark 1:32,34, emphasis added). Jesus didn't heal everyone, just as He won't heal everyone for whom you pray. However, there's an important difference here: Jesus healed everyone for whom He prayed, but He didn't pray for everyone who needed healing.

## CONDITIONS FOR HEALING

Many people think that the promise in James 5:15, "the prayer of faith shall save the sick," is a universal promise that anyone and everyone will be healed when we pray. But if this were the case, why don't we just walk through the hospital ward and pray the prayer of faith over everyone? And why are some people healed when we pray in faith while others are not? If we are to categorically claim that "the prayer of faith shall save," we must categorically meet the condition in the context of that promise as given in the fifth chapter of James. Let's examine some of these conditions.

1. *The elders of the church must be called.* First, the sick person must call for the elders of the church (the leaders of the local assembly) to pray for healing (see v. 14). This means that the people who exercise the prayer of faith are the spiritual leaders of the sick person (see Heb. 13:7; 1 Tim. 5:17), which assumes that there is a spiritual relationship between the one who is praying and the one who is sick. God seems to tie healing to the prayers of church leaders. Maybe some people who pray for healing don't get results because they leave out the local church.

2. *Any connection between the sickness and sin in the sick person's life must be examined.* James 5:15 states, "the prayer

of faith will save the sick, and the Lord will raise him up. And if he has committed sins, he will be forgiven." This suggests that the sins of the patient are connected to his or her sickness. In 1 Corinthians 11:29-30, Paul also makes a similar statement when he connects illness (and even death) in the church with those who had sinned at the Lord's Table. This ties back in to the first condition: A church leader would probably know about sin in the sick person's life and be equipped to deal with spiritual restoration before dealing with the physical sickness. Perhaps many prayers for healing are not answered because the sin issue has been neglected.

3. *The sick person must confess his or her sins.* Confession of sin appears to be another condition for healing: "Confess your trespasses to one another, and pray for one another, that you may be healed" (Jas. 5:16). So, before healing can occur, the sick person must acknowledge any sin of neglecting God or walking away from Him that might have caused the illness.

4. *Don't forget about the judgment of God.* James introduces his section on the prayer of faith with a warning: "lest you fall into judgment" (Jas. 5:12). Sometimes, illness may occur in a person as a result of a consequence of sin and the judgment of God. In such cases when a person's sin is being punished, the intercessor must first deal with the sin issue.

Interestingly, the Greek word used in this passage for "prayer" is *proseuchomai,* which, as you may remember from chapter 1, implies face-to-face contact with God. So, this type of prayer is not one in which we are asking God to heal or are making strong demands and begging God to bring healing. Rather, prayer for healing implies a relationship with God—the sick person must turn his or her face towards God and come back into fellowship with the heavenly Father.

## OBSERVATIONS ABOUT HEALING

As we observe these conditions set forth in James' letter and pray for healing, we need to remember a few important points. The following are 10 important things to consider when asking God to bring healing:

### 1. Don't Demand
God may not heal the way we ask or the way that we expect. People do not usually immediately get out of bed, nor does the fever immediately break. Since one of the basic premises is that the body heals itself, God may answer our prayers by removing the disease in the body—but it will still take time for the person to regain his or her strength through sleep, food and exercise.

### 2. Keep It Simple
Healing prayers do not have to be involved petitions or long, drawn-out requests. God does not hear us because of how long we pray, or how boldly we pray, or how we word our prayers. A straightforward and simple prayer is like one person asking for help from another: "Will you help me?" God's answer is simply, "Yes."

### 3. Pray to Bring Strength
Sometimes the sickness is psychosomatic, which means that the sick person doesn't really have the disease they fear; they only

think that they're sick. Many people make themselves sick with their faulty thinking. However, when we pray in faith and boldly expect God to answer our prayers, the sick person can take strength from our intercession and become "healed" by our statement of faith.

### 4. Remember That God Is Always Involved

Healing is often related to God's timing, and He may be at work in the situation long before we become involved. Perhaps the sick person's fever has already run its course or the antibiotics in his or her system have already curbed the disease when God leads us to pray in faith, and healing occurs. God is timeless and "calls those things which do not exist as though they did" (Rom. 4:17). Long before we pray, God is involved in the process—our prayer may just be the culminating event at the end of a long process of healing.

### 5. Lay Hands on the Person

Laying hands on the sick person is an important outward symbol that is taught throughout the Bible. When we lay hands on a sick person, our faith releases power for healthy living or healing. On many occasions in Scripture, Jesus touched the sick when He healed them (see Mark 6:5; 8:22-25), and Paul did the same (see Acts 28:8-9). However, it is important to remember that it is not the laying on of hands that brings healing but that the healing comes through Christ working in us.

### 6. Ask Questions

We should always ask questions before we pray. If we jump into praying without first asking questions, we may pray the wrong way, for the wrong things, or at the wrong time. James warns us not to ask amiss (see Jas. 4:3). I learned this the hard way.

When I greet the people attending my Sunday School class, I also watch for empty seats so that I can find my absentees. I then phone my absentees during the week to tell them that I missed them and to ask how I can pray for them. I find that this is a great way to discover spiritual needs and dreams.

During one such phone call, a member of my class asked me to pray for her mother, who was dying. Without asking a question or listening, I glibly said, "We'll pray for her healing."

"No," the daughter responded, and then went on to explain to me the severe problems that her mother was having. She then requested that I pray for her mother to die easily and without pain.

I did pray for her mother, and shortly thereafter she did die without pain. But if the woman had not stopped me, I would have asked amiss for something that was not in the will of God. We need to always ask the person to identify their needs so that we can be sure that we are praying the right way.

## 7. Practice Listening

We should always practice listening to the sick person before we pray. A lot can be learned by listening: We may discover why the person is sick, what spiritual struggles he or she has, and how to best pray for that individual. When Jesus healed the man at the Pool of Bethesda, He first asked, "Do you want to be made well?" (John 5:6). Obviously, the man wanted to be made whole, because he was waiting at the Pool of Bethesda for an unseen angel to come and stir the water (see v. 4) The man responded to Jesus' question with an explanation as to why he had not been healed: "Sir, I have no man to put me into the pool when the water is stirred up; but while I am coming, another steps down before me" (v. 7). By asking questions and listening to the man, Jesus initiated hope in the man.

## 8. Strengthen Faith Before Exercising It

We must strengthen our faith before exercising our faith. It's kind of like a batter stretching to get his muscles loosened before he steps up to the plate, or a golfer taking a practice swing to train his swing. When I call my absentees in my Sunday School class, I usually ask two questions: "How can I pray for you?" which is a challenge to their faith, and, "What do you want God to do for you?" This helps me to pray specifically for the person but also stretches my and the other person's faith for what we expect from God.

## 9. Pray Out Loud

When we pray out loud with the person who is sick, we fulfill the conditions of James, who tells us to "pray for one another" (Jas. 5:16). The word for "pray" used in this verse is *euch*, which means to make a vow before God. So when we fulfill our vow in prayer, we say to God what we want Him to do. This is similar to the conditions that Jesus gave for prayer: "I say to you, whoever says to this mountain, 'Be removed and be cast into the sea,' and does not doubt in his heart" (Mark 11:23).

## 10. Be Specific

Finally, we need to be specific in our prayer requests to God. I call praying out loud *say-it-faith*.[3] When we say in prayer what we want, we stretch our faith to believe God for healing. Many people pray vaguely, saying, "Lord, bless this sick person." Obviously, God would bless that person by healing him or her, but when we ask for specific *healing*, we have exercised the prayer of faith.

# YOUR ASSIGNMENT

*Pray for a physical ailment that you have.* No matter what you plan to do about your physical problem, pray specifically about it. Now analyze what you've done. How do you feel about your prayer? What role do you think your prayer had in your recovery?

*Write in your diary how you were healed.* Make sure to include what role you think your prayer played in the healing process.

*Ask God to teach you how to pray for sickness.* As you request this from God, go back over this chapter and learn the principles of healing. When you know how God heals, you'll pray with much greater confidence.

**Notes**

1. Saint Augustine was the bishop of Hippo from 396 to 430, one of the Latin Fathers of the Church, one of the Doctors of the Church, and perhaps the most significant Christian thinker after the apostle Paul.
2. Augustine, *The City of God,* trans. Gerald G. Walsh and Daniel J. Honan (New York: Fathers of the Church, 1954), book 22.8, p. 445.
3. See Elmer Towns, *Say-It-Faith,* available online at www.elmertowns.com under the link "Books Online."

# when we are in despair

*Search me, O God, and know my heart; try me, and know*
*my anxieties; and see if there is any wicked way in me,*
*and lead me in the way everlasting.*

PSALM 139:23-24

Have you ever felt as if you were in a pit and God was not there? Have you experienced times when it seemed as if you were starving to death in a desert and you didn't know which way to escape? Or maybe you felt as if you were in a dark room and couldn't find the door? When you pray, you feel alone; when you cry out to God, it seems as if He is not listening. How did you cope?

Many people who encounter such situations and dark periods in their life retreat into *introspective prayer*. Instead of reaching upward, they turn inward. They complain . . . and they gripe . . . but mostly, they blame themselves. As a result, they end up feeling even more hopeless, discouraged and depressed than they did before. In this chapter, we will examine some of the causes and problems associated with introspective prayers and determine if they have any benefit to our lives.

## THE CAUSES AND EFFECTS OF INTROSPECTION

Job is perhaps the best example in the Bible of a person who prayed introspective prayers. Job did nothing wrong, yet he was a victim of violence, theft and bankruptcy. He experienced incredible hardship and suffering—his cattle were stolen in a raid; his sheep and servants were killed in a fire from the heavens; his sons and daughters were killed when a house fell in on them; and his camels and other servants were killed in a different raid (see Job 1:13-19). Time and again, Job cried out to God for deliverance. Soon, Job began looking within himself. He complained to God and blamed himself for his misfortunes.

Introspective prayer is always rooted in fear. After Job's health was also taken from him, Job cried out, "For the thing I greatly feared has come upon me, and what I dreaded has happened to me. What strength do I have, that I should hope?" (Job 3:25; 6:11). Introspective prayer is also always focused on self-blame and self-pity, as Job also experienced:

> Is there not a time of hard service for man on earth? Are not his days also like the days of a hired man? Like a servant who earnestly desires the shade, and like a hired man who eagerly looks for his wages, so I have been allotted months of futility, and wearisome nights have been appointed to me. When I lie down, I say, "When shall I arise, and the night be ended?" For I have had my fill of tossing till dawn (7:1-4).

What is the result of praying introspectively in this manner? Utter hopelessness. When Job looked at his situation, he complained, "My days are swifter than a weaver's shuttle, and are spent without hope. Oh, remember that my life is a breath! My eye will never again see good" (Job 7:6-7). Job's wife expressed much the same sentiment when she said to Job, "Do you still hold fast to your integrity? Curse God and die!" (Job 2:9).

There will be many times in this life when we will feel abandoned by God and lose hope, but the truth is that we're never alone. God is present everywhere at the same time. Jesus has promised, "I will never leave you nor forsake you" (Heb. 13:5). The Lord is always with us—the problem is that we don't always feel that He is there. What blocks our communication with God and makes us feel as if He is not present?

Sometimes it's a knowable sin in our life that we won't come to grips with that blocks our relationship with God. Sometimes it's an unknowable sin. At other times, we may not feel God's presence because we are focused only on ourselves . . . our needs . . . our plans . . . and our pains. We become so involved with our own situation that we don't see God's hand guiding our daily affairs.

Sometimes it's not sin in our life but a wrong decision that we have made. Perhaps we came to a fork in the road and knew that God wanted us to take the right path, but we decided to ignore God's instruction and turned left. Maybe this is why the One in heaven is silent. He doesn't tell us that we chose the wrong road—He lets us find out through the consequences we suffer. We can't expect Him to come again to tell us which road is right, because He already told us once before. And if He did speak, would we really listen to Him the second time?

Sometimes it's not sin or disobedience that is the problem but just the fact that we have become inattentive. Maybe God wanted us to help someone, but we were too busy with our own affairs. Or maybe God wanted to say something to us, but we weren't listening. The only way God can get our attention in such situations is to stop talking until we're ready to hear from Him. By compelling us to become introspective in our prayers, we can then begin searching within for answers.

## INTROSPECTION BRINGS SELF-KNOWLEDGE

Seen in this light, the prayer of introspection does produce one incredible benefit—self-knowledge. It's a wonderful gift to understand what we *can't* do in this life; it's an even better gift to know what we *can* do. Blessed is the man or woman who knows the limits of his or her spiritual abilities!

The foundation of self-knowledge that we gain in introspection can become the foundation on which we build the rest of our lives. When we build on correct knowledge about ourselves, we can then make corrections, additions or deletions in our life. When we act properly on the self-knowledge that we have gained, we build holistic spirituality.

However, if introspective prayer is the *only* way we pray all of the time, we'll soon end up in trouble. We'll end up feeling defeated because we will become tangled up with sin in our hearts. We'll end up feeling discouraged because we will only see our failures. We'll always end up punishing ourselves for actions that we have taken or decisions that we have made. When we honestly look within ourselves, we will not like what we see. Paul looked at his life introspectively and cried out, "For the good that I will to do, I do not do; but the evil I will not to do, that I practice. Now if I do what I will not to do, it is no longer I who do it, but sin that dwells in me" (Rom. 7:19-20). We should never let our prayer of introspection be self-introspection alone.

How many times have we gone to the doctor and told him or her what we thought was the problem, only to have the doctor find an entirely different problem after a full examination? Our disease may be caused by something entirely different from what we originally thought. Sometimes the doctor must take decisive action to save our life or prescribe medication or exercise to change our circumstances. The point is that we must take decisive action to seek out expert medical advice when we are in physical pain. In the same way, we must seek out a divine diagnosis when we are "shut up" in introspective anguish.

When we take an introspective journey into our innermost parts, we should always take God with us so that we can see what He wants us to experience. The psalmist said, "Search me, O God, and know my heart; try me, and know my anxieties; and see if there is any wicked way in me" (Ps. 139:23-24). When we become introspective, we need to make sure that we look at ourselves through the eyes of God. Why? Because God reveals to us what we need to see and shields us from things we shouldn't see.

For our own good, God doesn't show us every wicked thing in our hearts, for if He did, we would be overwhelmed. Paul took that journey and concluded:

> I don't understand myself at all, for I really want to do what is right, but I don't do it. Instead, I do the very thing I hate. I know perfectly well that what I am doing is wrong, and my bad conscience shows that I agree that the law is good. But I can't help myself, because it is sin inside me that makes me do these evil things" (Rom. 7:15-17, *NLT*).

## INTROSPECTION AND REPENTANCE

How do we feel when we reach the end of a prayer of introspection? Usually discouraged or depressed. Paul expressed this feeling after a time of introspection when he cried out, "O wretched man that I am! Who will deliver me from this body of death?" (Rom. 7:24). Praying introspectively is like going into a dirty, smelly bathroom; the experience is unpleasant, so we leave.

So what do we do when the prayer of introspection leaves us down in the dumps? When the Israelites sinned, they brought a sacrifice to God, and we can do the same thing. We can bring our lives as a sacrifice to God and allow the blood of Jesus Christ to cleanse us from all sin (see 1 John 1:7). The prayer of introspection should bring us to the place of cleansing.

Forgiveness gives us a new beginning and allows us to start all over again. But we can't just ignore the sin that we find during our times of introspection. We must deal with it honestly—through repentance—and then turn away from that sin. We must turn away from our depression or failures and ignore anything else that we find in the prayer of introspection. And after we learn the truth about ourselves, we need to use that knowledge to build a new life and a better future.

# Your Assignment

*Use introspection properly.* You will become introspective at times, but always use it for the purposes of finding your problems, and then ask for forgiveness in the blood of Christ. Don't allow yourself to become entangled in only focusing on your failures and short-comings and end up praying prayers of introspection all the time.

*Claim God's victory.* After your time of introspection, embrace *victory prayer* and claim God's triumph over any depressing thoughts. Begin praise praying, in which you thank God for everything in your life. You will eventually end up at worship prayer, in which your thoughts will be centered on God and not on your problems. Isn't balance the key to everything?

*Live each moment in the presence of God.* When you're caught up in introspective prayers, you stop worshiping God. So make it a point to focus on God and His presence, not on your aches and pains. Let God's strength control your life.

# when we engage in spiritual warfare

*And so it was, when Moses held up his hand, that Israel prevailed;*
*and when he let down his hand, Amalek prevailed.*

EXODUS 17:11

Moses stood on the high peak, watching the battle unfold before him on the plain. Israel was being attacked by the evil nation of Amalek—a people who had hated Yahweh and the Israelites for 400 years and who would continue to fight Israel for the next 1,000 years. As the battle spread out on the plain before Moses, it was not just sword against sword and physical strength against muscle. The battle raging below was one of spiritual warfare. It was the kingdom of light against the kingdom of darkness, God against Lucifer.

As long as Moses held up his hands in intercession to God, Joshua and the Israelites prevailed. But the battle was a long one, and Moses grew tired keeping his hands extended. But when he lowered his hands, the Amalekites began to prevail in the battle. What could be done?

> But Moses' hands became heavy; so they took a stone and put it under him, and he sat on it. And Aaron and Hur supported his hands, one on one side, and the other on the other side; and his hands were steady until the going down of the sun (v. 12).

With Moses' arms now propped up, Joshua was able to win the battle against the Amalekites. The point of the story is clear:

When intercessors engage in warfare prayer, God's people are victorious. It was only when Moses lacked his prayer partners that the enemy rushed in to overwhelm the forces of God. But there is another important lesson to be learned as well: When we can't prevail in prayer by interceding on our own, God sends others to help in the intercession. There is power when two or more people gather together in prayer (see Matt. 18:19).

## SIGNS OF SPIRITUAL WARFARE

Spiritual warfare often begins when as an internal distraction while praying. We may find ourselves warring with ourselves to overcome distractions, laziness or idle thoughts, or against temptation, lust or evil influences that may surround us. Sometimes the presence of evil can be felt in the surrounding atmosphere like moisture on a foggy day—there is no rain present, but our faces still get wet because of the mist that is present in the air. When we feel the presence of evil distracting us from intercession in this manner, we can (1) have an outright confrontation and rebuke the demons, (2) stand against the power of demons, or (3) claim the supernatural power of Christ as we wrestle against the distractions.

Sometimes when we are trying to pray, we may feel distanced from God and unable to converse with Him. It's like trying to talk to someone on an airplane, but the announcements over the loudspeaker keep distracting us from the conversation. There have been times in my life when I have had such strong distractions that I had difficulty focusing on prayer. There have been times when I was tempted to think about something other than God. I have to struggle just to keep my mind focused on what I am praying.

So what can we do when we face this initial form of spiritual warfare? First, we can focus all our mental energy on what we are praying. When that doesn't work, we can ask God to help us overcome the interruption. There have been times when I have prayed, "God, help me keep my mind on my topic so I can pray." We can also change the environment. I often change positions, pray while standing up, and walk around my office instead of praying in one spot to avoid distractions. Sometimes I even walk through every room of our house as I wrestle to "get through" to God with my prayers.

We can also use symbols such as baptism, the Lord's Table and the cross as tools in our spiritual warfare. When the Israelites fought against the Amalekites, Moses stood on the top of the hill with the rod of God in his hand (see Exod. 17:9). Moses had to extend the rod as a symbol of God's power in the lives of the Israelites. Of course, sometimes the tools we need are more practical in nature—such as a pew to sit on at church or a rug on the floor where we kneel so that our attention in prayer is not diverted.

## AN AGGRESSIVE RESPONSE

Satan may try to put evil thoughts into our minds when we are praying. He might even be so crafty as to try to get us to pray for something that is sinful. When this happens, there are courses of action that we can take: (1) we can read Scripture out loud (reading out loud tends to keep our minds on what is being read); (2) we can pray out loud; (3) we can write out our prayers (see chapter 24).

Martin Luther once saw a manifestation of Satan on a wall while he was praying. Obviously, this type of distraction interrupted his prayers. Luther retaliated by throwing an ink bottle at the manifestation of Satan, splashing ink over his office wall in the process. That's one form of spiritual warfare!

The greater the intrusion from satanic forces, the greater the response from the intercessor needed to counteract that intrusion. Some intercessors rebuke Satan outwardly. I prefer not to do that (although I don't criticize those who do) but instead pray out loud, "Lord, I pray against this evil that is trying to direct my thoughts from You." Personally, I don't like the idea of talking to the evil one—I'd rather talk to God about the problem.

A Christian woman in Atlanta, Georgia, faced bankruptcy and humiliation because of undisciplined spending habits in her family. One day while she was walking through a department store, she noticed a purse and was tempted to purchase it. She began thinking that she needed the purse and then started to rationalize that with a new purse, she could take pride in her spending habits and discipline her money.

Suddenly, the woman realized that she was being tempted by Satan. So she yelled out loud, *"Get away from me, Satan!"* A nearby saleslady said, "I beg your pardon?" for she misunderstood what was being said. Now, I don't suggest that we should verbally rebuke the devil or yell at him, but the point is that when Satan is assertive in his temptation, we need to be equally aggressive.

## THE CYCLE OF SPIRITUAL WARFARE

Moses' and the Israelites' victory over the Amalekites occurred when Israel was crossing the wilderness toward the Promised Land. When the people of Israel entered the desert, they began to grumble because Moses had not supplied them with water. The thirstier the people became, the more they complained. Finally, Moses cried out to the Lord and said, "What shall I do with this people?" (Exod. 17:4).

In answer to his prayer, God told Moses to take his rod and smite a rock in a place called Horeb. "Behold, I will stand before you there on the rock in Horeb; and you shall strike the rock, and water will come out of it, that the people may drink" (v. 6). When Moses obeyed, water instantly gushed out of the rock. The people drank and rejoiced because of the physical deliverance that God had provided—but they also understood that this was a spiritual victory. They shouted, "Is the LORD among us, or not?" (v. 7, *NIV*).

In the desert, water is more precious than money. After God gave this blessing to His people, the Amalekites attacked Israel to get the water rights of Horeb. What this should tell us is that when we receive a great victory or a great answer to prayer, we should rejoice but not go on a spiritual vacation. Spiritual attacks are most likely to come against us when we have received blessings from God.

Because we are creatures of habit, most of us tend to wrestle with the same problems all of our lives. Some of us have constant money problems, some give in to temptations of the flesh, and others struggle constantly against drugs, depression or alcohol. Amalek represented that type of recurring enemy to Israel. The people of Amalek fought Abraham over water rights 400 years earlier, and they continued to battle against Israel for years. In fact, God told Moses, "The Lord will be at war against the Amalekites from generation to generation" (v. 16, *NIV*). God understood that the battle against the Amalekites was over, but the war was far from won. Evil would continue to attack His people, so they needed to constantly struggle for victory.

Since life is a journey, we need to be continually in warfare prayer. We will never quit struggling until we arrive at our destination. We should forget about winning a once-and-for-all victory in this life or about obtaining a perfect tranquility in which we never have to engage in warfare prayer again. Victories typically lead to counterattacks by the enemy, so our next prayer challenge may be even greater than past prayer challenges.

Notice that in Israel's case, the first problem was to find water in a dry, hot and dusty desert. They faced the threat of dying from thirst. But when the people of Amalek attacked, the

Israelites faced an even greater threat—being slaughtered by an old enemy. We need to remember that when we defeat Satan on one day, he will return on a different day and in a different way to tempt us even more strongly in another area of our life. Be ready!

## PARTNERS IN PRAYER

The Watchers were a group of intercessors who prayed for Charles Spurgeon, the famous Baptist preacher at the Metropolitan Baptist Tabernacle in the late 1800s. Because of these intercessors, the Tabernacle became the world-class megachurch of the time, and Spurgeon and his congregation were able to plant churches throughout England and send missionaries around the world.

A small parlor table with six or seven chairs was located in the basement of the Tabernacle right under the pulpit. Every time Spurgeon preached, the Watchers would kneel on pillows next to their chairs at the parlor table and intercede so that God would give Spurgeon great power. Just as Joshua couldn't have won the battle without the intercessors on the hill, so Spurgeon would not have had worldwide influence without the Watchers.

When we engage in spiritual warfare, God will bring prayer partners into our lives to help us combat the attacks of the enemy. He will use people according to the gifts that He has given to them—Joshua and the soldiers fought the battle with the sword, Moses used his ministry of spiritual intercession to prevail on the Israelites' behalf, and even Aaron and Hur helped in their unique way. We must recognize our spiritual giftedness and serve according to our abilities.

What disrupted Moses' intercession? The disruption did not come because Moses lost interest in praying or that God did not answer. Rather, the disruption occurred because Moses' hands grew tired and he was too weary to keep them raised. He needed help to support his hands because was not physically able to hold them up for the duration of the battle.

In the same way, *we will need physical help when we are interceding to God.* As long as we have human bodies, we will encounter problems. We will get sick and need our friends to intercede for healing; we will struggle against temptation and need our friends to intercede in warfare prayer for us; we will face other physical limitations as we serve Christ in our respective mission fields and need our friends to pray in faith for healing. And sometimes we just won't be able to keep our eyes open. In the Garden of Gethsemane, Jesus told His tired and sleepy disciples, "Keep alert and pray. Otherwise temptation will overpower you. For though the spirit is willing enough, the body is weak!" (Matt. 26:41, *NLT*).

Who won the victory against the Amalekites? No one single person. Moses, Aaron, Hur, Joshua and the army of Israel all played a part in winning the battle. The best way for us to fight our spiritual battle is also with companions by our side. Companions give us an extra set of eyes to watch for the enemy and can watch our backs. Companions intercede *for* us and *with* us. Praying with prayer companions enables us to pray out loud and focus our attention on the battle. Winning the spiritual battle is a team effort, and without companions, we will not obtain victory. As Paul noted, "We are God's fellow workers; you are God's field, you are God's building" (1 Cor. 3:9).

Have you been attacked lately on either a spiritual or physical front? Gather your companions and launch your counterattack with warfare prayer. When you defeat the enemy, rejoice in God's deliverance and remember the victory that the Lord has given to you. After Israel won its great victory over Amalek, God told Moses, "Write this for a memorial" (Exod. 17:14). It is important that we keep records to remind ourselves of God's great answers to prayer.

# Your Assignment

*Actively battle against distractions.* Pray out loud so that you can better focus on your requests or write out your prayers on a sheet of paper. Sometimes, I trace each prayer request that I have written down. I find that the physical movement of my finger helps me to stay focused on praying for each item.

*Pray with your eyes open.* When you close your eyes, it's often easy to "think" and not focus on your requests. However, when you open your eyes, don't look at something that would further distract you. I find it best to look out the window at trees and mountains. If I'm in a motel room or office without windows, I look at a wall or something else that doesn't distract me.

*Change your prayer posture.* When you feel distracted in prayer, experiment with changing your body position so that you can refocus your attention on prayer (see chapter 8). Try kneeling before the Lord, standing with your arms outstretched, folding your hands and bowing your head, or even lying prostrate on the floor.

*Know your weakest area.* The enemy knows your weak points and will attempt to attack you in those vulnerable areas. You don't need to write down your weak points, but be aware of them, pray about them, and strengthen those areas.

*Pray against your enemy.* Some call this "rebuking the enemy." When you pray against the enemy, do so cautiously, for our enemy has great supernatural power. However, feel free to pray boldly, because God has even greater power (see Matt. 10:28). If you sense an attack from the enemy, try praying out loud, claiming the power of the blood of Christ over the enemy. When I feel attacked, I often pray, "Lord Jesus Christ, protect me by Your blood. I claim Your power to resist evil, and I stand for You."

*Be ready for a counterattack after a great spiritual victory.* In order to demoralize you, the enemy will often attack right after you have scored a major spiritual victory. If you are aware of this tactic, you will find it easier to defend yourself against it.

*Seek help.* Just as Moses prayed for Joshua in battle, you need someone praying for you in battle. Just as Aaron and Hur helped Moses in his intercession, you need help when you intercede for victory. For more information, see my book *Prayer Partners,* available at www.elmertowns.com (click on the "books online" link to download a complete manuscript).

# PART 3:
# A BETTER CONNECTION

*How to Grow and Deepen Our
Relationship with Our Heavenly Father*

In this final section, we will focus on some of the more
complex matters regarding prayer, including meditation in
prayer, resting in prayer, vowing in prayer, praying in the Spirit,
and prayers of crucifixion. We will examine the often-
misunderstood topic of continually praying and will also look
at hypocritical prayers and written prayers. In the final chapter,
we will conclude by exploring the incredible transforming
power that prayer has in our lives.

# praying continually

*Rejoice always, pray without ceasing, in everything give thanks;*
*for this is the will of God in Christ Jesus for you.*

1 THESSALONIANS 5:16-18

When the Early Church was first established, the members, "continuing daily with one accord in the temple . . . ate their food with gladness and simplicity of heart, praising God and having favor with all the people" (Acts 2:46-47).

On several occasions, Paul instructed believers to pray constantly. To the Romans, Paul wrote, "Be glad for all God is planning for you. Be patient in trouble, and always be prayerful" (Rom. 12:12, *NLT*). To the Ephesians, Paul wrote, "Pray at all times and on every occasion in the power of the Holy Spirit" (Eph. 6:18, *NLT*). To the Colossians, Paul exhorted, "Devote yourselves to prayer with an alert mind and a thankful heart" (Col. 4:2, *NLT*). And to the Philippians, Paul wrote, "Don't worry about anything; instead, pray about everything" (Phil. 4:6, *NLT*). But Paul was not alone in exhorting Christians to be in constant prayer. Jesus told His disciples, "Men ought always to pray, and not to faint" (Luke 18:1, *KJV*).

So certainly this is an important principle in the Bible. But what does "pray continually" really mean? Does it mean that we are to intercede constantly in the presence of God? If that's true, it wouldn't leave much time for us to talk with our spouses, teach our children, or perform our duties in the work world.

## PRAY WITHOUT CEASING

Some people suggest that praying without ceasing doesn't necessarily mean that we have to pray all of the time but that we should remain in the "spirit" of prayer. It's kind of like the churchgoer who remains in a constant state of reverence when he or she is inside the sanctuary . . . continually quiet and serene. Again, this doesn't leave much time for having fun with our kids, cheering at a sporting event or fellowshipping with our friends.

Perhaps it would be helpful to look more closely at the phrase "pray without ceasing." The Greek phrase "without ceasing" does not mean "without stopping"; rather, it means "intermittently."

My wife recently bought a new car with an intermittent speed for the windshield wipers. When the rain is falling in a light mist, the wipers turn on automatically to clear the windshield at a slow pace. However, when the rain is pouring down, the wipers rapidly swish back and forth to enable my wife to see through the sheets of rain. In the same way, we are to pray *intermittently*. Sometimes we will pray lightly and softly, as when the mist is falling from the sky. But at other times our prayers will rush out of our heart in a rapid and frenzied manner, as when a heavy rain is pouring down.

Perhaps a better illustration would be the crying habits of a newborn infant. When something bothers a baby, he or she cries heavily and continuously. But the baby does not cry unless he or she is hungry, wet, or needs love and attention. In other words, the baby cries according to his or her *needs* at the time. In the same manner, we are to pray intermittently according to our needs.

Yet there is another point to consider regarding continual prayer. In Romans 8:16, Paul states that "the Spirit Himself bears witness with our spirit that we are children of God." A little further on in the same chapter, Paul writes:

The Holy Spirit helps us in our distress. For we don't even know what we should pray for, nor how we should pray. But the Holy Spirit prays for us with groanings that cannot be expressed in words. And the Father who knows all hearts knows what the Spirit is saying, for the Spirit pleads for us believers in harmony with God's own will (Rom. 8:26-27, *NLT*).

Whether we realize it or not, *prayer is going on continually* in us through the indwelling of the Holy Spirit. This works a bit like the electricity in our house. We do not have power until we plug in our appliance to the wall outlet; but once we do, the power is instantly available for us to cook our food, warm our room, or crank up our stereo. In the same way, the Holy Spirit dwells within us and constantly prays for us, and at any moment we can plug ourselves into His constant stream of prayer—at whatever level meets our needs.

I cannot tell you that I constantly pray or even that I am continually in the spirit of prayer. But I am frequently amazed at just how much I do pray throughout the day. Quite often, I find myself praying while I am driving. I find myself praying while I am waiting in line or when I am between duties at Liberty University. Almost always when a student asks me a question in class, I pray for wisdom so that I might give him or her the right answer.

When I "pray without ceasing," I'm not sure whether I'm grabbing hold of prayer or whether prayer is grabbing hold of me. I just know that it works when I constantly yield to the Holy Spirit.

## PRAY FOR THE LITTLE THINGS

Most of us live in a dichotomy. We have big spiritual projects for which we earnestly pray and seek God's intervention, but we ignore the humdrum or minutia. We pray, fast and beg God to move the mountains that block our way, but we ignore the little pebbles scattered in our path. What is the result? We see little connection between the little things in life and our spiritual walk with God.

Praying continually means talking to God about *every* aspect of our life—including the little things that we may think are unimportant to God. Many of us think that these little details have no connection to spirituality, but that's a wrong assumption. It's the small pebbles that get into our shoes that make it impossible for us to climb over the mountains. It's the small pebbles that accumulate and grow until they form the mountains that block our progress. There is a well-known saying that states "the devil is in the details," but the truth is that God is in the details. He works His will through the little things in life.

Consider the way that the Son of God entered into this world. God only had *one* Son, yet Jesus certainly did not enter the world in a "big" way. He was born in a little-known town called Bethlehem and in a little-expected place—a stable. He was born to parents who were obscure on the world's stage and unknown to anyone outside of their little village—parents who were travelers on a voter's registration roundup (see Luke 2:1-7).

When the Son of God was born, an angel of the Lord appeared to a group of shepherds in the nearby fields and told them that the promised Messiah had been born. To find the Savior, the angel told the shepherds to look for two small details: "You will [1] find a Babe wrapped in swaddling cloths, [2] lying in a manger" (Luke 2:12). The shepherds were not directed to a spectacular palace; the baby didn't shine with a holy radiance (as Jesus later did on the Mount of Transfiguration); there were no heavenly spotlights to point out the child. The identification marks were almost imperceptible to the uninstructed eye: God's Son would be wrapped in strips of cloth, lying in a feeding trough. How's that for *minute details*?

But isn't this the way that each of us truly discovers God? Just as the shepherds found Christ in the ordinary rudiments of life, don't we also discover God hidden in the minutia of life? Most of us just don't see God when we use the cell phone, grab a quick hamburger or fill the car with gas. We go through life ignoring the reverence of God in the little things in life. But the truth is that if we can't see God in the mundane routines of our daily life, we probably won't be able to see Him in the big celebrations or when the spotlight shines on us.

We need to get away from the idea that prayer is some ecclesiastical experience where we contemplate the abstract and realize that the true function of prayer is to bring us into a continual relationship with God. We need to see God in our mundane routines, because when we do, things such as stapling reports, cleaning the kitchen counters or buying groceries becomes a spiritual experience instead of boring drudgery. The difference begins in our perception and expectation. And isn't all life about perception and expectation?

## PRACTICING GOD'S PRESENCE

When I was a freshman at Columbia Bible College, I once heard a chapel speaker talk about Brother Lawrence, a seventeenth-century French monk who served in a monastery. The chapel speaker described how Brother Lawrence actually "practiced the presence of God" by continually practicing God's presence while he was washing pots and pans in his monastery's kitchen.[1]

The possibility of sensing God's presence wherever I went made a profound influence on my life. So I followed the example of Brother Lawrence. Even when I am caught up in the hustle and bustle of life, I have a private sanctuary in my heart into which I retreat. In my own little private sanctuary, I can practice the presence of God when I am sitting in a boring committee meeting or when I am caught in a traffic gridlock. When I walk through the crowds on campus, I can experience the presence of Christ that is just as real as if I had slipped into a secluded sanctuary in which the presence of God is most evidently felt.

In my own experience, I have found that it is much easier to practice the presence of God when I begin my day by consciously spending time with God in prayer. My commitment to be there with God activates a strong discipline within me to focus my mind on God. But just setting the time aside isn't enough—I know that to truly experience the presence of God, I must barricade myself against thinking about business activities or all the things I plan to do that day. It takes energy to meet God, and it only occurs as a result of a dedicated will to make it happen.

But there is a second step beyond discipline. For once we make the decision to seek God's presence, we begin to develop intimacy through regular association with God. We soon find that we desire to develop a habit of practicing God's presence in our life. Just as a person develops a *taste* for a certain food, we develop a *spiritual hunger* for God.

So what is "praying without ceasing"? It's developing *holy habits* to make our prayer life easier. Well, "easier" may not be the correct word—maybe it's making prayer more spontaneous or more natural. And in the process, we also make our godliness more practical.

## A CONTINUAL RELATIONSHIP WITH GOD

Just as a vine grows naturally and steadily up the garden wall, our ability to pray unceasingly won't come with a single experience but will grow naturally in our heart. A growing vine needs the energy of sunshine, the nurture of good soil and the intermittent refreshment of rain. Unceasing prayer also needs energy, nurture and refreshment, but most important, it needs discipline.

A girl who is learning the rudiments of playing the piano undoubtedly understands that it will take years of practice before her fingers will dance over the piano keys. But if she sticks with it and maintains good discipline, that girl—when an adult—will be able to play from deep within her heart. It will be a true art form. In the same way, discipline in prayer is key—we can know all about prayer, but the only way to develop unceasing prayer is to constantly practice it.

Constant prayer is not something that can be *taught*; rather, it is something to be *caught*. No one can teach us how to talk to God—it's developed from our intimate relationship with Him and our commitment to meet with Him each day. As God shows us how to live, we talk to Him. As God shows us what not to do, we talk to Him. As we face the constant needs and difficulties in life, we talk to Him.

By continually talking with God—even if it's just a few sentences at a time—we learn that God can be intimate and personal. And through this constant communication—continual prayer—the relationship and intimacy between us and our heavenly Father grows.

# YOUR ASSIGNMENT

*Make a choice to be a person of prayer.* Prayer is not just something that you do in the morning. Make prayer an absolute necessity throughout your daily life. Decide to make a one-time choice to continually talk to God, and then each day tap into the power of that choice.

*Begin the day with prayer.* Begin each day by talking to God in a conversational manner. Over time, you'll discover that you will be able to naturally talk to God in unceasing prayer throughout the day.

*Memorize Scripture.* Memorize the following verses to help you pray throughout the day:

- *O God, You are my God; early will I seek You; my soul thirsts for You; my flesh longs for You in a dry and thirsty land where there is no water* (Ps. 63:1).

- *Watch and pray, lest you enter into temptation. The spirit indeed is willing, but the flesh is weak* (Matt. 26:41).

- *Rejoice always, pray without ceasing* (1 Thess. 5:16-17).

*Ask God for help.* If you don't seek to meet with God in prayer, it won't happen! So ask God to help you meditate on Him and talk to Him throughout the day. This is a prayer that God can answer and wants to answer.

**Note**
1. Brother Lawrence, *The Practice of the Presence of God: With Spiritual Maxims* (Grand Rapids, MI: Fleming Revell, 1999).

# CHAPTER TWENTY

# meditation in prayer

*Let the words of my mouth and the meditation of my heart be acceptable in Your sight, O LORD, my strength and my Redeemer.*

PSALM 19:14

When you think about mediation, the first image that probably pops into your mind is that of practitioners of Eastern or New Age religions reciting mantras and contorting their bodies into odd positions. Meditation in Christian prayer and worship is something that most of us don't ponder or discuss with our friends on a regular basis; but the truth is that the practice is found in many places throughout Scripture.

My good friend, Stan Toler, a Nazarene preacher in Oklahoma City, Oklahoma, begins every day by reciting Psalm 19:14—"Let the words of my mouth and the *meditation of my heart* be acceptable in Your sight, O LORD, my strength and my Redeemer" (emphasis added). Every day, Stan prays that his words will glorify God and that his meditation will be acceptable to God. What greater prayer could any of us say to God?

What is meditation? *Webster's Dictionary* states that the word "meditate" means "to focusing one's thoughts on: to reflect on or ponder over; to plan or project in the mind."[1] While that is a secular definition, it at least points us in the right direction. But *Christian meditation* is very different from the practice that is performed in Eastern and New Age religions. In Eastern religions, the deeper practitioners go into meditation, the more they lose their identity.

The practitioners meditate in order to merge with a "cosmic consciousness" so that they live another life from their normal ones.

Biblical meditation has the opposite purpose. Rather than losing our identities to some cosmic consciousness, we obtain a clearer view of who we are as individuals before God. When we meditate on God and Scripture, we grow stronger and are motivated to act on what we've been thinking. Christian meditation is the ability to hear God speaking to us and understand what He is saying. Perhaps a better definition of "meditation" is "thinking God's thoughts after Him."

Christian meditation begins when we hear God's voice through His Word and realize that He is speaking to us. It continues as we ponder what God's Word means and what He wants us to do with our lives—and then flows out into our spirit as we repeat what God has said. The purpose of Christian meditation is to hear what God is saying to us, to know for certain what God wants us to do, and then to *do* it.

When we practice Christian *meditation*, we're actually following the command that God gave to Joshua:

> This Book of the Law shall not depart from your mouth, but you shall *meditate* in it day and night, that you may observe to do according to all that is written in it. For then you will make your way prosperous, and then you will have good success (Josh. 1:8).

Notice that Joshua was commanded to *meditate* on God's Word both day and night. When Joshua did this, God told him that he would prosper and have good success. Since one of the best ways to learn meditative prayer is to look at how people meditated in the Bible and then follow their example, let's examine some other biblical examples of meditation.

# MEDITATING ON DELIVERANCE AND
# THE GREATNESS OF GOD

As a young shepherd boy, David often thought about nature as he tended his sheep in the great outdoors (see Ps. 23). As he observed and pondered the wonder of God's creation—the sun, the moon, the stars—he was in absolute awe of His Lord. "The heavens declare the glory of God; and the firmament shows His handiwork," he declared (Ps. 19:1). As David observed God in nature, he also meditated on what he saw: "Let the words of my mouth and the meditation of my heart be acceptable in Your sight, O LORD, my strength and my Redeemer" (v. 14).

David was eventually elevated to the king of all Israel. When he became king, David brought the Ark of the Covenant into Jerusalem, set up the Tabernacle so that people could worship God, and appointed a man named Asaph to reestablish the nation's worship. Asaph had an interesting history and connection to David. During the 13 years that David hid out in the wilderness to escape King Saul, Asaph hid out right alongside him. Had Saul caught David, Asaph would also have been killed.

Yet if we look deeply into Asaph's character and at the 12 psalms he wrote, we find a man of immense gratitude. Asaph realized just how many times he had almost been caught and killed by Saul and gave thanks in meditative prayer for all of his past deliverances: "I will remember the years when the right hand of the Most High helped me. I will remember the things the Lord did for me in the past. I will meditate on Your words when I am in trouble" (Ps. 77:10-12, *ELT*).

It's often uncomfortable for us to think about the past, especially when we contemplate how close we came to failure or death. Asaph often had similar difficulty in meditating on his past:

"When I thought how to understand this, it was too painful for me—until I went into the sanctuary of God; then I understood their end" (Ps. 73:16-17). However, many times in Scripture we are exhorted to remember both the good *and* the bad things of life, for recalling our past is an important aspect of meditative prayer. In the end, we should always remember "that all things work together for good to those who love God, to those who are the called according to His purpose" (Rom. 8:28).

## MEDITATING ON THE PRESENCE OF GOD

When David began organizing different tasks to reestablish worship in the nation of Israel, he appointed much of the ministry of song to a group of people known as the Kohathites. Included among the members of this group was a musical family known as the sons of Korah (see 1 Chron. 6:31-33).

Korah was the head of a priestly family back in the days of Moses. Korah had probably felt the sting of the whip when he was a slave in the land of Egypt, but he (along with the other Israelites) had been delivered when the Lord's Angel of Death passed over Egypt. Korah had walked through the Red Sea on dry land and witnessed the miraculous power of God.

Korah had started out by following the leadership of Moses, but over the course of the journey he became dissatisfied with his position—in other words, he got a bit too big for his britches. When Korah demanded that he be allowed to share leadership with Moses, God instructed Korah to come to the Tabernacle. But Korah refused. Can you imagine refusing to obey God and refusing to go to the Tabernacle? This act of disobedience didn't go over well with God—the earth immediately opened up and Korah and the other rebels were swallowed up. God had judged Korah and his followers.

The death of Korah had an indelible and continual influence on his sons, grandsons and great grandsons. The sons of Korah determined not to be rebellious like their father. They stayed in the Tabernacle, as close to God as possible, and wrote great psalms as they meditated on their intimacy with God. They had a passion for the presence of God and meditated on His ways: "My soul longs, yes, even faints for the courts of the LORD; my heart and my flesh cry out for the living God. Even the sparrow has found a home, and the swallow a nest for herself, where she may lay her young—even Your altars, O LORD of hosts, my King and my God" (Ps. 84:2-3).

## MEDITATING ON THE CONSEQUENCES OF DISOBEDIENCE

After the Babylonian captivity, the prophet Haggai returned to the Promised Land with the other exiled Israelites. The people soon began rebuilding the Temple of God, but after a time, construction on the Temple stopped. Haggai delivered a sermon to motivate the Israelites to finish building the Temple. He told the Israelites that they should consider the fact that they were disobeying God: "Now therefore, thus says the Lord of hosts: 'Consider your ways!'" (Hag. 1:5).

To consider something is yet another way to meditate on God. Haggai went on to tell the Israelites that they should meditate about the consequences of their disobedience and think about the glory of the previous Temple: "Who is left among you who saw this Temple in its former glory?" Haggai asked. "This house doesn't compare with it at all" (2:3, *ELT*)

Furthermore, Haggai reminded the Israelites that they needed to consider what God would ultimately do with the Temple that they were reconstructing: "The glory of this latter house will be much greater than the former" (2:9, *ELT*). The gold and silver that lined the Temple of Solomon would not compare to the glory of the Temple that they were now building, for Jesus—the glory of God—would walk into the very Temple that they were constructing.

## MEDITATING ON CHRIST

When Jesus was born in Bethlehem, Mary and Joseph were visited by a group of shepherds who told them what the angels had proclaimed to them about their Child. All who listened to the shepherds marveled at what they had to say, but Mary "kept all these things, and pondered them in her heart" (Luke 2:19). To ponder in this sense means to remember or think about the past. These were not just idle thoughts passing through Mary's mind, but rather intentional and focused meditation.

Mary's meditation centered on the baby to whom she gave birth and the little boy whom she would raise. Mary knew that Jesus had been conceived by the Holy Spirit and witnessed the many miracles that surrounded His birth. So what did she do? She constantly meditated on the human Jesus.

Mary's meditation is similar to what young people ask today: *What Would Jesus Do? (WWJD?)* Asking this question requires us to stop and contemplate how the human Jesus would act in a situation similar to the one we are confronting—and then act the same way. Paul also reminds us to think as Jesus thought: "Set your mind on things above, not on things on the earth" (Col. 3:2). We are to meditate on the person of Christ, who stands victoriously in heaven for us. "If then you were raised with Christ, seek those things which are above, where Christ is, sitting at the right hand of God" (v. 1).

## MEDITATING ON THE LOVE OF GOD

The apostle John was the youngest of the twelve disciples. After Jesus was arrested in the Garden of Gethsemane, John followed Jesus as He went through His trials and then followed Him to the foot of the cross, where Jesus was crucified. As John witnessed the suffering and slow death of his Lord, he heard Jesus say, "Behold your mother!" (John 19:27). Because of the cross experience, John took care of Mary for the rest of her life.

As an older man, John often meditated on the cross experience. "Behold what manner of love the Father has bestowed on us, that we should be called children of God," he wrote (1 John 3:1). For John, "beholding" meant meditating on how deeply Christ loved him—a love so strong that Christ would offer to die for his sins (see 1 John 4:9). John realized that the *agape* love of Jesus was self-sacrificing love. The cross not only represented the death of Jesus but was also a reflection of the Father's love.

What was the result of John's meditation? He felt overwhelmed to be considered a child of God. "Beloved," he wrote to his fellow believers in Christ, "now we are children of God" (3:2).

## MEDITATING ON THE GIFTS OF GOD

Can you think of a more intimidating task than to be the pastor of a church that both the apostle Paul and the apostle John had pastored before you? A young man named Timothy found himself in this position when he became the pastor of the church in Ephesus, one of the greatest churches in the apostolic world.

I imagine that Timothy's mind was filled with fear. He probably worried that he wasn't up to the task. Perhaps this why Paul wrote to Timothy and told him to remember God's calling for his life and the spiritual gifts God had given him. Basically, Paul told Timothy to just be himself:

> Do not let your youth stop you from fulfilling your call from God, but be an example by your words, love, faith, purity, and good spirit. Keep on teaching and preaching

doctrine. Don't neglect the spiritual gifts God has given to you . . . meditate on your calling and gifts; give yourself wholly to them (1 Tim. 4:12-15, *ELT*).

The focus of meditative prayer is to continually grow to be more godly in character and action. A man and wife become like one another the more that they talk and relate, and the same is true of God and us. We can't become God, nor can we ever become perfect as God is perfect, but we can become godly—we can become Godlike. We can constantly talk with God and meditate on Him, knowing that when we do, we please Him.

Remember, Christian meditation is not becoming one with the universe, as in many Eastern religions and New Age meditation. Rather, it is us as created beings focusing on the glory and majesty of our Creator. Our relationship with God is intended to be a relationship of two conscious beings who are in constant communication with each other. There is no loss of identity in Christian meditation—no merging of two personalities into one entity.

We will never be able to fully master meditative prayer, but we can grow in our ability to talk with God. I remember a hymn from my childhood that reflects this idea well: "And He walks with me, and He talks with me, and He tells me I am His own, and the joy we share as we tarry there; none other has ever known."[2] As we walk and talk with God and meditate on His ways, we develop our relationship with our heavenly Father. And the joy that we will experience in His presence is like nothing that we can experience here on Earth.

# YOUR ASSIGNMENT

*Speak your concern to God and listen for His response to your inward heart.* Just as you can't force yourself to go to sleep, you can't force meditative prayer. When you try too hard to *meditate*, you attempt to control God, which can't be done. Remember that meditative prayer is *communion with God*. After you speak to God, listen to what He has to say to you. Meditative praying is intimate conversation with God—and that simply can't be manipulated.

*Ask God for a deeper desire to talk to Him.* While you can't force yourself to fall asleep, you can create conditions that will allow sleep to happen. It's the same with meditative prayer. The first criteria for initiating a conversation with God is to have a deep desire to meditate on God and talk with Him. Isn't that the first criteria for initiating a conversation with anyone?

*Listen.* Stop talking to God and listen for His voice. You won't hear an audible voice, but you will hear God speaking to your heart.

*Become quiet before God.* In order to listen to God and hear His voice, you have to be still before God. Use the following questions to guide your meditation:

- As you read God's Word, what is He saying to you through the Scriptures?
- Are you living in the Word?
- What is God saying to you through His laws of nature?
- Are you living within the divine principles of life?
- Are you listening for the voice of God in all circumstances?
- Is God speaking to you through failure?
- Is God speaking to you through success?

- When severe consequences hit you, do you feel the judgmental hand of God, or do you believe that it is nothing more than circumstantial?

*Ask God for His presence.* When you feel God's presence, you will be in a much better state to meditate on Him. How do you feel His presence? *If you worship the Father, He will come to receive your worship.* The Lord's presence will fill your sphere of living because "the Father seeks worship" (John 4:23, *ELT*).

*Internalize what you are reading, feeling and experiencing.* When you study the Bible, determine what it means to *you.* When you meditate on the Word, determine how it applies to *you.* Basically, the written Word of God must become the living Word of God in your heart.

*Accept what you read.* All too often we try to analyze the Word of God to learn what it means—and that is not necessarily wrong. However, meditative prayer should not be cerebral or mechanical, but visceral—we *touch and feel* the truth of God.

**Notes**

1. *Webster's Dictionary*, 11th edition, s.v. "meditate."
2. C. Austin Miles, "In the Garden," 1868-1946. http://www.webedelic.com/church/inthegart.htm (accessed October 21, 2004).

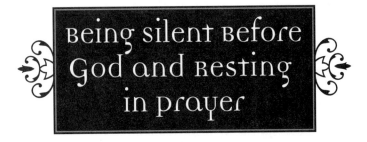

Being Silent Before God and Resting in Prayer

*So there is a special rest still waiting for the people of God.*
HEBREWS 4:9, *NLT*

In the previous chapter, we mentioned that in order to listen to the voice of God, we first have to be quiet before God. In today's world, that can be difficult to accomplish at times. We have over 100 channels on our TV sets that blare programs and commercials throughout the day—and DVD players and TiVo to record anything that we might have missed. We can chat with others online (even people we don't know) and communicate to anyone in the world through e-mail. And of course, we carry cell phones with us that allow us to talk with our friends at any time of the day.

But does "more" communication necessarily mean "better" communication? Do greater opportunities to communicate directly corollate to receiving more meaningful content? In fact, the opposite appears to be true. We communicate more but say less than ever before. Why is this? Because we are empty within. We have very little to say, so when we listen or read we have very little with which to interpret what we take in.

Are we addicted to words? Are we compulsive talkers? What about our prayer life? Do we pour out an abundance of words to God? Probably not. Even when we talk a lot to God, we are usually asking Him for things . . . a solution to a problem . . . some money . . . to change someone else.

David wrote, "I wait quietly before God, for my salvation comes from him" (Ps. 62:1, *NLT*). What does it mean to wait quietly or silently before God? It means to *rest* in the presence of God and wait for Him to speak to us and to manifest His presence. We don't ask for anything, nor do we strive in intercession. We rest not because we're tired—even when we're physically exhausted—but because we just want to be in the presence of God. We quit striving and worrying and just enjoy the peace that being in the presence of God brings.

## THE POWER OF SILENCE

Do you know that there is power in silence? The power of silence comes not from the absence of words but from presence of God. When we are silent before God, the Lord can heal us, or build us up, or make us what He intended for us to be: "My soul, wait silently for God alone, for my expectation is from Him" (Ps. 62:5).

Being still and resting in God's presence pleases our heavenly Father, for when we control our words, we also control our thoughts and actions. James wrote, "No one can tame the tongue. It is an uncontrollable evil, full of deadly poison" (Jas. 3:8, *NLT*). Our words reflect the anger in our hearts, reveal our sin, project our greed and tell everyone that we are selfish and vain. But when we control our words, we become the disciplined people that God want us to be: "But those who control their tongues can also control themselves in every other way" (3:2, *NLT*). Silence reflects the beginning of our self-discipline and reveals that we are a follower of God.

Silent or "wordless" praying is a learned art and a skilled discipline. There is a difference between art and skill: Art comes naturally, while skill must be developed through training and repetition. The art of silence comes from within because our renewed souls passionately seek the presence of God. The discipline of silence, however, is something that we must constantly practice and strive to obtain, because it is natural for us to want to talk. But when we finally learn silence, we will begin to know and relate to God.

Silence is difficult because often it may seem as if nothing is happening. We sit and rest in silence, waiting to hear from God . . . and grow impatient when the words don't immediately come. But does communication only occur through words? Think about two people in love. They may not say a word—or even be thinking anything substantial—but by their very silence they communicate love, contentment and happiness to each other. It takes a long time to fall so deeply in love with someone that this type of communication is possible. In the same way, it takes a long time to learn to successfully pray without words.

Silent prayer can also be difficult because it reveals the attitude of our hearts. When we come silently to God, He shines the light of His glory into our souls and we realize that we can't offer any excuses for our failures or rationalize away our sin. In the silence, we comprehend that He knows everything about us and that there is nothing we can hide from Him. Silence forces us to receive conviction for our sins, criticism for our actions, and correction for our bad decisions. But as we examine our hearts in our silence, God reveals how we can change our lives and become better people. And we will find rest in God.

## SILENCE AND SALVATION

John Wesley, the famous Methodist preacher, decided to commit his life to the Lord after listening to a reading of Martin Luther's preface to Romans at a meeting on Aldersgate Street, London. He later recounted his experience:

> In the evening, I went very unwillingly to a society in Aldersgate Street, where one was reading Luther's preface to the Epistle to the Romans. About a quarter before nine, while he was describing the change which God works in the heart through faith in Christ, I felt my heart strangely warmed. I felt I did trust in Christ, Christ alone for salvation; and an assurance was given me that he had taken away my sins, even mine, and saved me from the law of sin and death.[1]

Notice that Wesley states that his heart was "strangely warmed" but doesn't tell us what he prayed to get saved—or even that he prayed at all. His conversion was not centered around prayers made up of words but rather reflected the experience of his heart.

An old Methodist preacher who I once knew used to say "I know that I know that I know" when asked about how he was certain that he was a child of God. Why did he say "I know" three times? Well, he knew in his *head* that he was saved because he read it in his Bible. He knew in his *heart* that Christ had saved him because he had experienced Jesus coming into his life. And the old Methodist preacher just innately knew *deep inside* that he was a child of God. It was a comprehension deeper than mere head knowledge, or emotional feelings, or even words. Just as the preacher knew that fire was hot and water was wet, he knew that he had been forgiven.

Most of us don't like to talk this way because we have been taught not to base our salvation on our feelings. But this knowledge that comes from deep within represents more than just feelings—it represents *faith* in God. Feelings and facts may waver, but faith will never slip. Faith is an assurance that God places deep within our hearts.

The aged apostle John reinforced this concept when he stated, "I write this to you who believe in the Son of God, so that you may know you have eternal life" (1 John 5:13, *NLT*). So, silent prayer may be a fact of expressing faith. When we come silently into the presence of God, by faith we know where we are and in whose presence we stand. By faith, we're not blown about by every wind of doctrine or by every storm of emotion (see Eph. 4:14-15). We know that the world, the flesh and the devil are out to get us, but we stand silently in the presence of God and upon the Word of God.

## THE IMPORTANCE OF REST

One of the pitfalls of having 100 channels on our TV, internet access and cell phones is that we're always tempted to engaged in some form of activity. We're tempted to always be on the go, always pursuing our own agenda. Perhaps we worry that if we don't work seven days a week, we won't have enough money to meet our needs. Or maybe we've just become so accustomed to being active all the time that we can't picture any other way of life. Or maybe our parents taught us that we should be working all the time, and now that thought process is deeply ingrained within us. Silence before God seems awkward and uncomfortable, so we refuse to just *rest* in God's presence.

Why is it important to rest? For that matter, why did God include a day of rest in the Ten Commandments that He gave to the Israelites when He took them out of Egypt?

Remember the Sabbath day, to keep it holy. Six days you shall labor and do all your work, but the seventh day is the

Sabbath of the LORD your God. In it you shall do no work: you, nor your son, nor your daughter, nor your male servant, nor your female servant, nor your cattle, nor your stranger who is within your gates (Exod. 20:8-10).

Obviously, God intended for *every* Israelite to obey this command to rest—even their cattle had to rest! But *why* is it important to rest? Perhaps the next few verses from Exodus explain the reason: "For in six days the LORD made the heavens and the earth, the sea, and all that is in them, and rested on the seventh day" (v. 11). We *rest* because God first rested. Genesis 2:2 states, "On the seventh day God ended His work which He had done, and He rested on the seventh day." God rested on the seventh day, which is the last day of the week. We call this day the "Sabbath" because the Hebrew word for rest is *Shabbath*. But why would God *need* to rest?

God wasn't physically tired after creating the world. He is omnipotent, which means that He has the power to do all things that are possible. He has the energy to accomplish anything that is imaginable. God certainly didn't need *physical* rest. He also wasn't emotionally stressed out after Creation, because creating the universe wasn't too much for God, nor did it contain more details than He could handle. God didn't need *emotional* rest. And God didn't need a vacation to revitalize His focus. Sometimes we go away for the weekend because we need a change of pace. Because we are finite, we need a change of vision and new goals to keep us going. But God isn't a finite being. He didn't need to rest to get a new perspective after creating the world.

God rested because He had finished all that He had intended to do. He had spoken all things into existence, His Word had breathed life into a lifeless clay man, and that man had become a living soul. God *rested* because Creation was complete. And just as God rested after He was finished, He wants us to enjoy that same experience.

## THE SONG OF THE SABBATH

Every song, regardless of how intricate it is or what style of music it represents, eventually comes to a conclusion. In the same way, we should "sing" the "song of work" until it comes to a conclusion at the end of the week and then pick up the rhythm of the "song of the Sabbath." In the rhythm of that song, we worship God, pray, learn more about Him, and replenish our souls so that we can again pick up our work for the next week. If we choose to work all the time, we miss out on this incredible opportunity to sing with God.

Did you catch that? God *sings*. The Bible teaches, "He will rejoice over you with singing" (Zeph. 3:17). Since God sings, why not learn His song and sing with Him?

The problem is often that we feel God is enslaving our spirits. We don't recognize God's music and don't want to sing His song. We feel that the Sabbath is a theological system filled with regulations and laws that steal our freedom. So we dismiss the Sabbath as mere legalism. We refuse God's *rest*.

But God didn't intend for us to just be inactive on the Sabbath. We still work on the Sabbath, but we work for different purposes and with different people. Most people who go away on vacation still engage in some type of physical activity. Often, that physical activity is even more strenuous than what they do in their 40-hour-per-week job, but it still renews their spirit because it is a different kind of activity.

During the week, our tendency is probably to take control of everything with a firm hand to make things happen. We believe that in order to get ahead, we have to run . . . fight . . . block the enemy . . . and persevere. Often, we apply the same strategy to praying. We think we must attack every problem with aggressive prayer . . . warfare prayer . . . struggling prayer . . . never-give-up prayer. We pray with all of our might, just as during the week we work with all our might.

But on God's Sabbath, we sing God's song. The music is different, the words are different, the rhythm is different, and even the chords are different. Singing is singing, whether we are singing at work or in the home—so singing God's song may take as much physical activity as it takes to sing our work song. But when we sing God's song, we enter into the Sabbath rest. We no longer take things into our own hands but instead rest in God's divine hands. Jesus said, "Come to Me, all of you who labor and are heavy laden, and I will give you rest" (Matt. 11:28). We get Sabbath's rest when we come into the presence of God.

There are two things to keep in mind about the Sabbath. First, keeping the laws of the Sabbath will never make us spiritual. Getting into a right relationship with God does not mean creating a bunch of rules and then forcing those rules on ourselves and others. In the Bible, the Pharisees tried to impose their laws on Jesus when Christ attempted to heal a man on the Sabbath. "Is it lawful to heal on the Sabbath?" they exclaimed (Matt. 12:10). Jesus replied, "What man is there among you who has one sheep, and if it falls into a pit on the Sabbath, will not lay hold of it and lift it out? Of how much more value is a man than a sheep? Therefore it is lawful to do good on the Sabbath" (vv. 11-12).

We can't find the presence of God by just keeping the law. The whole purpose of the Sabbath is to enjoy the presence of God. But there's another important point to consider about the Sabbath— rest is *good* for us. It wasn't God's intention to punish us when He told us to keep the Sabbath day holy. Nor did He intend to be a selfish dictator who wanted to keep us from having fun on His

Sabbath day. No! God knows we need *rest*. He knows we'll get more done on the six days of work if we rest for one day. He knows that we'll find more happiness by finding His presence on the Sabbath. Sabbath rest is good and good for us. Enjoy.

## REST AND BE STILL BEFORE GOD

On the seventh day, God rested. The music of Creation ended and God sang a different song. We need to make sure that we have our Sabbath rest so that we can set God singing. If we don't plan our daily time with God, we'll miss the serenade. Isn't that enough motivation to rest each day in God's presence—to hear Him sing?

And let's quit trying to force our way into the presence of God. We don't have to bang on the door or yell to get God's attention. Too often we think of silence as the absence of noise or just nothing in the room. But silence is something. Silence has its own existence. Just as God exists as a being without a physical presence, so silence exists for us. When we enter the stillness of our personal sanctuary, we'll find that God is there. He is waiting for us in our silence.

# YOUR ASSIGNMENT

*Try bowing in God's presence without talking to Him.* Paul admonishes us to "aspire to lead a quiet life" (1 Thess. 4:11). Ask God to help you learn the lessons of quietness. God can both teach you to be quiet and give you quietness.

*Examine the reasons why you have trouble becoming quiet before God.* For some people, it's hard to sit silently. Why? There are many reasons why we may constantly want to have noise around us or be continually engaged in conversation. We may be afraid of the unknown or what the light of God will reveal in our lives. We may be unaccustomed to silence, so it is awkward for us. We may be impatient and not want to wait to hear God's voice. Examine some of these reasons in your own life.

*Determine to listen for God's voice.* Commit to spending a few minutes of your quiet time each day just listening for God's voice. Don't talk, pray or read the Bible—just listen. "For thus says the Lord GOD, the Holy One of Israel: 'In returning and rest you shall be saved; in quietness and confidence shall be your strength'" (Isa. 30:15).

*Yield your legalistic ideas about rest to God.* Forget about rules when you meet each day with God. Don't look at your watch. Turn off your cell phone. Since "Sabbath" means "rest," just quietly rest in His presence.

*Let God talk to you through His Word.* One of the best ways to rest is to read the Word of God, listen to the Word on CD, memorize the Word, or meditate on the Word. Become focused on God's Word and you'll find rest in Him.

*Listen for God's messages in meditation and communion.* When you are silent before God, something's happening that you don't realize. Your body is resting from the pressures of work and your daily life. Your spirit is being rejuvenated from the stresses it faces in the world. Your mind is being recreated with the image of God so that you can better recognize, think, understand and know. Don't you need God's rest?

**Note**

1. John Wesley, quoted in Harry Uprichard, *Son Is Revealed: Discovering Christ in the Gospel of Mark* (Faverdale North, Darlington, England: Evangelical Press, 1999), n.p.

# vowing in prayer

*But I will sacrifice to You with the voice of thanksgiving; I will
pay what I have vowed. Salvation is of the LORD.*

JONAH 2:9

Hannah was a woman without children and caught in a stressful marriage. Her husband, Elkanah, was also married to another woman who constantly ridiculed Hannah because she was barren. So Hannah decided to go into the Tabernacle to search out the presence of God. As Hannah wept in anguish from the bitterness in her soul, she made a *vow* to God that if He would give her a son, she would dedicate that son to God's service.

> Then she made a vow and said, "O LORD of hosts, if You
> will indeed look on the affliction of Your maidservant
> and remember me, and not forget your maidservant, but
> will give your maidservant a male child, then I will give
> him to the LORD all the days of his life, and no razor
> shall come upon his head" (1 Sam. 1:11).

Hannah believed that her prayers for a child were not enough, so she made a vow—a prayer of promise—to change her circumstances. She vowed that her son would live in the priestly community and not be raised at home with her. God heard Hannah's prayer and gave her a son, whom Hannah named "Samuel," which means "heard by God."

There is something significant about the vow that Hannah made. Notice that Hannah told God that if He gave her a son, "no razor shall come upon his head." In biblical times, people sometimes put themselves temporarily under a *Nazarite vow* to indicate to God the importance of their request and the level of commitment that they were willing to invest if God granted their petition (see Num. 6). Hannah, however, took this one step further by dedicating her son to a *lifetime* of service to the Lord. Samuel would become a Nazarite—one who did not cut his hair, go near dead bodies, or eat the grapes of the vine for the rest of his life.

The person who made such a vow was absolutely required to carry out the vow made before the Lord: "When you make a vow to the LORD your God, you shall not delay to pay it; for the LORD your God will surely require it of you, and it would be sin to you" (Deut. 23:21). And so, as difficult as it must have been, Hannah kept her vow and gave her son back to the Lord (see 1 Sam. 1:28).

## A LIFE-CHANGING DECISION

People often make vows to God when they get into trouble. "Lord," they pray, "if You will heal me, I'll quit getting drunk" or "Lord, I promise to become a missionary if You just get me out this mess." This type of prayer is not what we mean when we talk about a *prayer vow*. Vowing in prayer does not mean *bargaining* with God or saying, "I'll do something for God if He does something for me." No, vowing in prayer implies something much deeper—we vow to be faithful to God no matter what comes our way.

The prophet Jonah made a life-changing vow to God at some point in his difficulties. Perhaps this occurred during the storm at sea right before Jonah was thrown into the ocean. Although Scripture does not tell us exactly when the vow was made, there is no doubt that Jonah felt its effects. After Jonah was delivered from the belly of a great fish, he declared, "I will pay what I have vowed" (Jon. 2:9).

Jacob made a prayer vow in the dead of a night while he was on a journey. He was running from his brother, Esau, and was afraid. He laid his head upon a stone that he had picked up and had a dream in which he saw a ladder coming down from heaven. Angels ascended and descended the ladder, and the Lord was standing above it (see Gen. 28:11-13). When Jacob awoke, "he was afraid and said, 'How awesome is this place!'" (v. 17).

When Jacob awoke the next morning, he made a vow to God and said, "If God will be with me, and keep me in this way that I am going, and give me bread to eat and clothing to put on, so that I come back to my father's house in peace, then the LORD shall be my God" (vv. 20-21). Jacob, being the shrewd businessman that he was, didn't want to fully commit himself until God had met certain conditions. Yet God, in His grace, still accepted Jacob's vow. Jacob—in his own flawed way—had made a vow from that day forward to put God first in every part of his life.

Perhaps we—like Jacob—are standing at a fork in the road in which our decision will alter the course of our life. At such times, we may want to make a vow in the presence of God. Why? Because we want God—who knows the future—to guide our commitment and keep us from making a mistake. Beyond this, we want to dedicate our life to seeking God's perfect will (see Rom. 12:2). However, when we make such prayer vows, we need to be careful not to just bargain with God, as Jacob did. We need to completely commit our life to God without conditions or reservations.

## STRENGTHENING THE PRAYER VOW

Vowing in prayer is certainly not for the faint of heart. As indicated by the stories of Hannah, Jonah and Jacob, the prayer vow can involve making a decision that will forever alter our lives. The prayer vow is only for those who want to go deeper into the presence of God and completely commit to doing God's will. Actually, the prayer vow deals with our power of choice. Not only must we choose God, we must also choose to do what God reveals.

We should also be cautious before rushing into making vows in prayer. In the Sermon on the Mount, Jesus reminds us to be careful about making vows to God—especially if we are not in a position to fulfill them or have no intention of keeping them:

> I say to you, do not swear at all: neither by heaven, for it is God's throne; nor by the earth, for it is His footstool; nor by Jerusalem, for it is the city of the great King. Nor shall you swear by your head, because you cannot make one hair white or black. But let your "Yes" be "Yes," and your "No," "No." For whatever is more than these is from the evil one (Matt. 5:34-37).

Jesus seems to be saying that we should make no vows at all but just choose to live our life with integrity. However, on two separate occasions, the apostle Paul took vows on his missionary journeys. In Acts 18:18, Paul took a vow that resembled the Nazarite vows that Jews had been practicing for centuries: "So Paul . . . had his hair cut off at Cenchrea, for he had taken a vow." In Acts 21:20-26, Paul joined with four other men who had taken a vow and agreed to go through Jewish purification ceremonies in order to demonstrate to the Jewish community that he was not instructing people to turn away from the laws of Moses or adopt Gentile customs. Paul took this second vow, shaved his head, and even paid the fees for the whole group (see Acts 21:20-26).

The point is that making vows is permitted by God, but we need to be extremely cautious that we don't make unwise vows. Perhaps this is one reason why people choose not to make such vows. Maybe they made a commitment to meet God for 10 minutes each day but quit trying when they slept in late one day—and now they skip their devotions altogether. Since the past pledge was too heavy a burden for them, they don't want to risk making the same mistake again by saying another vow in prayer.

What should we do when we make such a vow and then trip up and fall? Simply get up and start following God again. We form a habit of obedience by simply obeying; so if we truly want to obey God, we need to get up and just start following Him again. Consider a little child who is learning how to walk. Yes, the infant falls down a lot, but there's something in the heart of little children that makes them get up and try again. The child will get up to start walking again—and then fall down again—and then get right back up again. If we have fallen and not fulfilled our vow, now is the time to get up and start walking again.

When we stumble in our walk with God, we can't just stay on the floor. We have to get past our spiritual inferiority complex, in which we tell ourselves, *I can't do it,* and past the personal condemnation that we level upon ourselves when we think, *I'm not good enough to do it.* Just as God puts an urge in little children to get up after they fall, so He puts within us an urge to get up and follow Him again. Our character is not measured by what it takes to knock us down but by our ability to get up each time we're knocked down.

Just as every disobedience weakens our will, every obedience strengthens our resolve. When we obey in small steps, we receive power to take larger steps in the future. So don't look for the perfect time or place to obey, because there won't be one. If you live in a dysfunctional home, it may never be convenient to obey

God, but do it anyway. If you are in a stressful job, you may never have the time to obey God, but do it anyway. If your private life is a mess, it may not be easy to obey God, but do it anyway. Your small obedience will give you a small inward peace, and each time you obey, the peace of God will grow to influence and direct your life (see John 16:33).

A reasonable place to begin might be to make a vow to be consistent in our daily quiet time with God. There is a common assumption that since prayer is so important, we will naturally do it, but it just doesn't happen that way. We all lead busy lives that tend to choke out prayer time. It's amazing how many "things" show up to interfere with our daily time with God. The phone rings, someone knocks at the door, or some other crisis occurs that calls for our immediate attention. When these outer distractions don't call us away, there are always inner distractions to contend with. Our minds will wander, we will suddenly remember something that we forgot to do, or while we're praying we'll get up from our knees to try and fix whatever we have been praying about.

Many of us try to manage our daily devotions; but the truth is that if we haven't made a vow to meet God daily at a regular time, it's hard to manage a commitment that's never been made. If we want to grow in our relationship with God, we need to put Him *first* in our daily schedule. If we want to succeed in prayer, we need to make a commitment to pray for a regular length of time each day. If we are at that place on a regular basis to worship the Lord, He will come to receive that worship.

# YOUR ASSIGNMENT

*Check your motives.* Remember that God loves you unconditionally and that fulfilling a vow isn't going to change the way that He feels about you. Make sure that when you make a prayer vow, you are not trying to bargain with God and that you are not putting yourself under a legalistic burden.

*Think about some past vows that you've broken.* This exercise is not to make you feel guilty but to prepare you for your next prayer vow. What are the reasons why you failed? If it was sin, confess it. If it was neglect, determine to do better next time. If distractions got in the way, make a *vow* to put God and His will first in your life.

*Begin with small or nonconsequential vows.* In one sense, there are no small vows, because many small ones add up to big experiences. But when you begin making vows, choose some smaller ones that you know you can fulfill. This will strengthen your commitment before you begin tackling the tougher ones. For example, some simpler vows to make might include

- meeting with God at a certain time each day
- spending a certain amount of time in prayer each day
- reading a certain amount of Scripture on a daily basis
- committing to keep a prayer list
- praying the Lord's Prayer each morning before you start the day

*Pray before making any vow.* Before making any vow, make sure that you are committing yourself to God's plan, and then pray for God to lead you to make only the vows that He would have you make. The main reason why most people break their vows is because those vows were made at the wrong time, for the wrong reason, or because they should never have been made in the first place. So it is important to carefully choose a vow that you know is in God's will.

*Remember your prayer vow to meet with God each day.* Your vow will compel you to commit to meeting with God each day so that you can reap the rewards of being in His presence. And once you are in God's presence, make another vow to commit to do those things that will enrich your life and make you profitable in God's kingdom.

# Hypocritical prayers

*And when you pray, you shall not be like the hypocrites.*
*For they love to pray standing in the synagogues and on the*
*corners of the streets, that they may be seen by men. Assuredly,*
*I say to you, they have their reward.*

MATTHEW 6:5

The word "hypocrite" comes from the Latin word *hypocrisies*, which was used to describe a person who gave a false appearance of having admirable principles, beliefs or feelings. The hypocrites in Jesus' day—typically the Pharisees—wore their religious garb out into the marketplace to show off their spirituality. They took the best seats in the Synagogue and sat at the head table at the banquets (see Mark 12:38-40). And to make sure they got their point across, they stood on the street corners with their hands lifted to God and prayed out loud so that everyone could hear them.

When Jesus delivered His sermon on the mount, He told the multitudes, "When you pray, you shall not be like the hypocrites. For they love to pray standing in the synagogues and on the corners of the streets, that they may be seen by men" (Matt. 6:5). Why did Jesus single out the hypocrites? Because hypocrites pray in order to develop a false façade. They pray in order to focus on themselves and obtain self-glory, robbing the Lord of the glory and honor that is due Him.

Sometimes God does not answer our prayers because we "pray amiss," or with the wrong motives (see Jas. 4:3). Have you prayed over someone and "puffed up" your prayer to make it sound good instead of just speaking from your heart? Have you ever tried to *look* spiritual to impress someone else? When we pray for things to make ourselves happy or in order to glamorize ourselves, we engage in *hypocritical prayer*.[1]

## THE WRONG REWARDS

The problem is self! We are all motivated by our pride. We want people to think that we are spiritual. But what did Jesus say about those who prayed for their own self-glory? "They have their reward" (Matt. 6:5). Hypocritical prayer is the most insidious motivation to prayer because it takes the focus off of God and places it on ourselves. In the end, our hypocritical prayers accomplish nothing more than making us feel a bit better about ourselves for a time. For as Jesus said, "Whoever exalts himself will be humbled, and he who humbles himself will be exalted" (23:12).

The root of the problem with hypocritical prayers is attitude. Instead of keeping our relationship with God private, we show it off to everyone. Now, it's not wrong for people to see us pray, nor is it wrong for us to pray out loud before men, nor is it wrong for us to pray on the street corner. The issue is always attitude—when we pray hypocritically, we try to look spiritual on the outside while feeding our flesh on the inside.

So there are two dangers with the prayer of hypocrisy. First, we tend to hide our pride behind a cloak of religiosity. We hide any hunger that we might have for God under an egotistical drive for spiritual recognition. Second, we seek the wrong reward for praying. We should be praying to develop a relationship with God and experience the reward of being in His presence—not the reward of receiving glory from the people who see us pray. When we pray to seek the esteem of people, we are hypocrites.

So does this mean that we should only pray in private? Should we only pray when no one knows what we are doing? Didn't Jesus say, "But you, when you pray, go into your room, and when you have shut your door, pray to your Father who is in the secret place; and your Father who sees in secret will reward you openly" (Matt. 6:6)? It seems as if Jesus is saying that we should not pray before men. But that is not the whole picture.

## LETTING THE LIGHT SHINE

Jesus was not saying that praying *in public* is wrong. He was saying that praying *to be seen by the public* is wrong. Jesus makes this same comment about having the proper motives for doing good works: "Take heed that you do not do your charitable deeds before men, to be seen by them" (Matt. 6:1). Actually, Jesus must have prayed in public—or at least prayed in the presence of His disciples—for they asked Him, "Lord, teach us to pray" (Luke 11:1). The fact that someone saw Jesus praying and then asked a question on how to pray implies that Jesus did not keep it hidden from view.

Jesus even implied that it was all right to receive public recognition for doing the right things when He said, "Let your light so shine before men, that they may see your good works and glorify your Father in heaven" (Matt. 5:16). Praying in public is certainly one of the ways to let our light shine before others. Jesus was not saying that we should conceal the good things we do, just that we should want other people to see what we do so that God may be glorified. The issue is the glory of God, not our personal glory.

Look at the issue more carefully. It's not *whether* we want others to see what we are doing, but *why* we want others to see what we are doing. When Daniel prayed, he went to an upper room and opened his windows towards Jerusalem in open defiance of a decree that no one should pray to any other god than king Darius (see Dan. 6:6-11). Daniel's public prayer was not an act of hypocrisy, but a statement that he would only glorify the one true God of Israel. So when outsiders find out that we have been praying—or that we have received answers to our prayers—that's not wrong. As a matter of fact, it is good when God uses our testimony to encourage others to pray or serve the Lord.

## A Fine Prayer

A New York newspaper reporter once described a Christian who offered prayer at a large religious gathering by saying, "That was the finest prayer offered to a New York audience." Did the reporter miss the point? If it was a fine prayer, it should have been offered to God, not to a New York audience.

Don't let the prayer of hypocrisy rob you of your Christian testimony. If you are a parent, let your children see you praying at meals. It's good for them to see God supplying your needs. If you work among Christians, let them see you praying so that they know you depend on God. Your public testimony may inspire them to seek God or to know Him better. If you are among unsaved friends, don't hide the fact that you believe in Christ and follow Him. Let your light shine out and demonstrate the love of God to everyone in your life.

# YOUR ASSIGNMENT

*Ask God to teach you to pray with the right attitude.* When the disciples saw Jesus praying all night on one occasion, they asked Christ to teach them how to pray. Do the same as the disciples: Ask God to teach you how to pray for the right things and with the right attitude.

*Keep your focus on God.* Are you guilty of seeking self-glory when you pray or of trying to appear superspiritual? It's easy to shift your focus away from God when you pray and relegate Him to second place. But do you honestly believe that God wants to be in second place in your life?

*Yield any reward you get from praying.* In Matthew 6:6, Jesus says, "Your Father who sees in secret will reward you openly." Learn to pray so that you don't need the applause of those around you. Pray for the applause of God.

*Make God your greatest reward.* One reward of praying with the proper attitude is that God can hear your prayer and grant your request. But there's a greater reward—God Himself. When you focus on God, you are rewarded with His presence. When you come to God, the greatest accomplishment in prayer is entering into His presence and having fellowship with Him.

**Note**
1. It's not wrong to feel happiness as a result of prayer. Obviously, when God answers, we rejoice and are satisfied. The key is that we shouldn't pray for an answer just to be happy, but that we should be happy when we receive an answer.

# Reciting written prayers

*And Jabez called on the God of Israel saying, "Oh, that You would*
*bless me indeed, and enlarge my territory, that Your hand would*
*be with me, and that You would keep me from evil, that I may not*
*cause pain!" So God granted him what he requested.*

1 CHRONICLES 4:10

The church that I grew up in was a Presbyterian church in
Savannah, Georgia, and every Sunday morning we worshiped
with a semiliturgical service. Something that always bothered
me about the way our church conducted its service was that
the pastor always read his prayer. I don't know why, but reciting written prayers just didn't sit well with me. When I accepted Christ as my Savior at age 17, I didn't change my mind
about recited prayers—if anything, my disdain for them inten-
sified.

In my mind, prayer was talking to God and therefore spontaneous, so I rejected anything that I perceived to be dead or formal. I wanted the reality of Jesus without any outward formulas
or external props. Many people I know currently share this same
mind-set that I used to have regarding written creeds, written
liturgy and written prayers.

In 1982, I had breakfast with Dr. David Yonggi Cho, pastor
of The Full Gospel Church in Seoul, South Korea, which is the
largest church in the world. I greatly respect Dr. Cho, so I asked
him how I could become more godly. Dr. Cho responded by

telling me to pray "the rounds" each day, which I immediately recognized to mean the Lord's Prayer. Dr. Cho told me, "When you pray the seven petitions of the Lord's Prayer, you've prayed for every area of your life, and you've also prayed in every way expected by God."

Praying the Lord's Prayer each day became my first experiment with using a written prayer during my prayer time. Now, when I awake at 6:00 A.M, I throw off the covers so I won't go back to sleep and pray the Lord's Prayer before I get out of bed. After breakfast, when I get to my quiet time, I again pray the Lord's Prayer. I find saying the prayer is an all-encompassing bridge that takes me into the presence of God. Like exploring the deepest ocean, it opens my eyes to new insights from the Lord and gives me a new vitality in my personal walk with God. I found that a Christian's beliefs and experiences are all contained in the Lord's Prayer.

## A SERVICE ON THE LAKE

In 1996, my wife and I took a riverboat trip from St. Petersburg to Moscow and were crossing the White Lake in northern Russia one Sunday morning. There were no church services planned, so a friend and I asked the captain if we could conduct a meeting aboard the vessel. The captain agreed and allowed us to hold the service in the dining room.

The service was announced over the loudspeaker, and soon Russian Orthodox, Roman Catholics and a variety of Protestants from the United States begin filling the room. I quickly realized that most people didn't bring a Bible with them on the trip, so I decided to preach from a portion of Scripture that would be familiar to everyone—the Lord's Prayer. After all, it was certainly familiar to me, for I was praying it each morning.

Despite the differences among the Christian believers in the room, the sermon was well received. That afternoon, I started to write *Praying the Lord's Prayer* to capture some of the ideas and thoughts that had been presented during that Sunday morning service.[1] When the book was published, I had the opportunity to speak with Billy Graham, and I asked him to give my book away on his telecast as a special gift offer. "Many unsaved people who watch your telecast pray the Lord's Prayer in church," I said. "This book could lead to their salvation." Billy Graham gave away a quarter of a million copies of the book in 1999.

About that time, *The Prayer of Jabez* became a bestseller, which meant that millions of Americans were now praying a written prayer. People's lives began to be changed as they prayed:

*O that You would bless me indeed,*
*And enlarge my territory,*
*That Your hand would be with me,*
*And that You would keep me from evil,*
*That I may not cause pain!* [2]

Just as poets can capture their feelings and experiences in words, so written prayers can capture the deepest yearnings of our hearts. Of course, when I stress the value of writing out our prayers, I do not mean that we should rule out all spontaneity or conversation in prayer. Written prayers can be very conversational, and there will always be spontaneity in our written words when we truly pour out our heart in prayer in supplication or worship. In fact, writing out our prayers makes us more spontaneous because it forces us to break some of the negative habits we may have formed by always verbalizing our prayers.

## VAIN REPETITIONS

When some Christians pray out loud, they drop their voices into a deep bass resonance, as if they were trying to sound like God. Other Christians raise their voices and yell out their prayers, perhaps because they don't feel their prayers will be heard unless they put more sincerity or articulation into their voices. Some people emphasize certain parts of their prayers so that those words or phrases will capture God's attention. But praying in this manner puts the focus on the form of the prayer instead of on God Himself.

Maybe Jesus was referring to weaknesses of spontaneous prayer when He spoke of those who stood on the street corners and used "vain repetitions . . . for they think that they shall be heard for their much speaking" (Matt. 6:7, *KJV*). Their desire to pray loudly so that others could hear them brought them self-glory and made them into hypocrites before God. As I read this passage, I get the impression that their spontaneous prayers were nothing more than vain repetitions in God's ears.

It's easy to fall into the habit of always praying for the same things in the exact same way. Remember the old proverb, "Familiarity breeds contempt"? As humans, we naturally fall into certain habits and can become so familiar with the words we use that our prayers lose their meaning. Writing out prayers breaks us of these habits and helps us to become more focused on the actual substance of our requests. Written prayer helps us to become better prayer warriors.

Writing out our prayers delivers us from self-centered religion. When we share our written prayers with others, we allow them to come into our world, kneel with us, and listen to the concerns on our hearts. Our prayers serve to bless them and strengthen the Body of Christ as a whole. When we gather together in fellowship and share our written prayers, it enables us to come into an agreement concerning our requests (see Matt. 18:19).

## A FEW DRAWBACKS

With all of the benefits of written prayers, I should point out that there are a few implied weaknesses when we begin reducing our heart's passion into words. For example, when God places a great burden on our heart, one of our reactions is to fall on our face before the Lord. That's hard to put into words. When the apostle John saw "One like the Son of Man, clothed with a garment down to the feet and girded about the chest with a golden band" (Rev. 1:13), he fell to his face as though he were dead. That's an experience that can't be reduced to writing.

Perhaps one of the greatest weaknesses of written prayers is that we sometimes read them without seeking to understand the meaning behind the words. We repeat verses without thinking about what we say or to whom we are praying. The whole process becomes rote, and when that happens, we destroy the very meaning of prayer.

This brings us to another problem. Every day we have new needs, and every morning we face different problems. There is no written prayer that we can pray that will be relevant to tomorrow's needs, just as there are written prayers that weren't relevant to yesterday's needs. Remember, today counts!

Writing out our prayers can also cause us to focus on grammar and syntax instead of on the meaning of our words. Some people worry that they aren't very good writers and that their words won't convey the intended meaning to God. But let me quickly say that God will never reject our prayers because of poor grammar and will never turn a deaf ear because we used the wrong words. As a matter of fact, Scripture says, "Your Father knows the things you have need of before you ask Him" (Matt. 6:8). Other people may judge us by our grammar, pronunciation or poor choice of words, but our heavenly Father is much more concerned about our heart.

## PSALMS AND OTHER WRITTEN PRAYERS

As I mentioned, one of the best ways to begin using written prayers is by reciting the Lord's Prayer each day. Another great source for prayers are the psalms, which were written by a variety of people both in times of great joy and in times of great suffering. The psalms were not just for the Old Testament saints—believers in the Early Church used such written prayers during their times of worship, as Paul indicates in his words to the Ephesians:

> Do not be drunk with wine, in which is dissipation; but be filled with the Spirit, speaking to one another in psalms and hymns and spiritual songs, singing and making melody in your heart to the Lord (Eph. 5:18-19).

Two other excellent prayers that have been used by Christians for centuries are the "Jesus Prayer" (also called the "Prayer of the Heart" by some Church Fathers) and the "Holy Spirit Prayer." The Jesus Prayer is a composite of several prayers given in the New Testament (see Luke 17:13; 18:14,38) that has been widely used, taught and discussed throughout the history of Eastern Orthodox Christianity. The prayer simply reads as follows:

> *O Lord Jesus Christ,*
> *Son of God,*
> *Have mercy on me,*
> *A sinner.*[3]

The Holy Spirit Prayer is also rich in New Testament language. This prayer reads:

> *O Heavenly King, Comforter,*
> *The Spirit of Truth,*
> *Who is everywhere present, and fills all things,*

*The treasury of blessing and giver of life,*
*Come and abide in us,*
*Cleanse us from every stain*
*And save our souls, O Good One.*[4]

So let's not be afraid to express our heart to God through written prayers, or be concerned that we won't be spontaneous enough for God. Let's not worry that we won't write something profound or that we won't get the words and grammar just right. We can't impress God anyway! And when we do write out our prayers, we should share them with those around us so that those people can support us in prayer for our needs and be strengthened in their faith.

# YOUR ASSIGNMENT

*Write out one of your prayers today.* If you are unaccustomed to expressing your heart through written words, don't just jump into this new experience and try to write out all of your prayers. Be selective. Begin by writing out just one or two prayers that are especially meaningful to you.

*Begin a file.* Once you've written a prayer, create a file so that you can find that prayer and use it again when a similar circumstance arises in the future.

*Read prayers written by others.* You can find written prayers in daily devotional books or in the prayer books of a liturgical church. As you read these prayers, try to connect with the author and understand what he or she is expressing to God through the prayer.

*Pray the Lord's Prayer.* Of course, one of the best written prayers is the one that Jesus taught to His disciples. Begin each day by reciting the Lord's Prayer and meditating on the meaning of Jesus' words.

*Pray the Psalms.* Read through some of the psalms in the Bible and pick out several that are especially relevant to the situation you are facing. Recite the psalm as a prayer to God from your heart.[5]

**Notes**
1. Elmer L. Towns, *Praying the Lord's Prayer* (Ventura, CA: Regal Books, 1997).
2. Bruce Wilkerson, *The Prayer of Jabez* (Sisters, OR: Multnomah Press, 2001), n.p.

3. The exact wording of the Jesus Prayer has varied from a simple form such as "Lord, have mercy" to the more common form listed in this chapter. The earliest known mentions of the prayer are in the first volume of the *Philokalia* by Saint Diadochos (A.D. 400-486) and in *Pros Theodolulon* by Saint Hesychios (c. A.D. 700-800). See Fr. Steven Peter Tsichlis, "The Jesus Prayer," *Greek Orthodox Archdiocese of America,* http://www.goarch.org/en/ourfaith/articles/article7104.asp; and "Jesus Prayer," *Wikipedia,* http://en.wikipedia.org/wiki/Jesus_Prayer (accessed January 2006).

4. The Holy Spirit Prayer is part of the "Trisagion Prayers," a set of ancient prayers that is said in Eastern Orthodox services and devotions. See "Trisagion," OrthodoxWiki, http://www.orthodoxwiki.org/Trisagion _Prayers (accessed January 2006).

5. See Elmer L. Towns, *Praying the Psalms* (Shippensburg, PA: Destiny Image Publishers, 2004), in which I have translated the entire book of Psalms from Hebrew into modern English and then put them into a form in which they can be used as personal prayer to God.

# praying in the spirit

*But you, beloved, building yourselves up on your most
holy faith, praying in the Holy Spirit.*
JUDE 20

We are told to walk in the Spirit, to minister in the Spirit, and to
be filled with the Spirit. But what does it mean to *pray in the Spirit?*

In Galatians 5:16, Paul writes, "Walk in the Spirit, and you
shall not fulfill the lust of the flesh." I think I understand what
it means to *walk* in the Spirit, because when I have yielded to the
Spirit, I have gone about my duties with zest, optimism and joy.
When I walk in the Spirit, there is a spring in my step and I think
three or four strides ahead of where I am. It's as though I have
already arrived at the place where I am heading. But does this
describe what it means to pray in the Spirit?

In John 6:63, Jesus says, "It is the Spirit who gives life; the
flesh profits nothing. The words that I speak to you are spirit,
and they are life." I also think I know what it means to *minister* in
the Spirit, because when I have yielded to the Holy Spirit, my
thoughts have been controlled by the Spirit and I teach what
Christ wants me to communicate. The Holy Spirit controls my
mouth and gives me words that I hadn't planned to say. When I
teach in the Spirit, students see biblical insights, or they think
God's thoughts, or they are lifted to new levels of communion
with God. But again, does this describe what it means to pray in
the Spirit?

# RELINQUISHING CONTROL

Over the years, I think I've learned a little of what it means to pray in the Spirit. When I yield to the Holy Spirit in prayer, I pray with more confidence, more joy and more assurance. When I pray in the Spirit, I enter the "prayer of faith" (Jas. 5:15, *KJV*), knowing that God will hear my prayer.

In Ephesians 5:18, Paul tells us to "be filled with the Spirit." Now, technically, the Holy Spirit came into our lives the moment we were saved, because when we invited one member of the Godhead into our life (Christ), we received all the members of the Trinity: the Father (see John 14:23), the Son (see John 1:12), and the Holy Spirit (see Rom. 8:9). Every person who has accepted Christ has the Holy Spirit already dwelling within him or her. But what Paul is really saying in Ephesians 5:18 is that we need to allow the Holy Spirit to *control* our lives. The problem is that many of us bottle up the Holy Spirit and don't let Him influence or guide our life.

Praying in the Spirit means more than just delivering the lines that God feeds to us from the throne room of heaven. When we pray in the Spirit, we pour out our feelings to God through the words that the Holy Spirit gives us. Our prayers are full of spontaneity, our words spring from the depths of our hearts, and our emotions flow from the expanse of our love. The Holy Spirit energizes all of our forces in prayer and, as a result, the Father answers our prayers to heal the sick, deliver us from danger, provide for our needs, and more.

When we pray in the Spirit, our minds don't drift into fuzzy ideas or become cluttered with a moist fog so that we can't think straight. No, the opposite is true—when we are filled with the Spirit, we are more focused and think more clearly. Our emotions are upbeat instead of fearful or sad. When we are filled with the Spirit, we are surrendered to the Spirit, and thus our will is committed to God.

We may feel detached from everything about us, and yet through the Holy Spirit, we are more connected to the Father than ever before. We feel calm because we are depending upon the Holy Spirit for results. We feel confident because it's no longer our responsibility to control our lives, but His. We feel free from self-doubt and fear. We feel energized because the Holy Spirit is focusing all our energy in prayer. We are at peace because we are no longer striving to make this happen—we're just letting it happen.

## KNOWLEDGE AND EMOTIONS

Some people think that the more they know about the Holy Spirit, the more they will feel His presence. They believe knowledge of the Holy Spirit will automatically lead to filling by the Holy Spirit. However, we never live in the Spirit by just thinking about *how* to live for Him. When the Spirit comes, He takes over everything. He speaks through our minds, stirs up our feelings, and is released by our will.

This is not to say that knowledge of the Scripture and the Holy Spirit is unimportant. There is a definite relationship between knowledge of the Bible and God and the filling of the Spirit. If we know the Bible well and are filled by the Spirit, the Holy Spirit is able to use our knowledge of the Word of God at a much higher level of competency. We can do more, be more, and pray more effectively because the Spirit works on and through the biblical knowledge that we possess.

On the other hand, if we do not know the Word of God (and thus do not know much about God Himself), when we yield ourselves to the Spirit, He will also speak to us—but not as well as He would like to speak. This is because the Bible is God's *Word* and the Holy Spirit speaks through it. If we haven't filled our heart and mind with Scripture, we will not be able to do as much for

God as another person can who is as equally surrendered to God but who is saturated with the Bible.

When the Holy Spirit fills us, He will use the Scriptures we already know to give us more insight into the mind of God. When we pray in the Spirit, our human spirit and the divine Holy Spirit work together as one. The Holy Spirit will make our emotions more expressive and accentuate our personality, but we won't become one with the Spirit and lose our identity. God is always God, and we are always human.

In my own life, I find that I am most in the Spirit when there is a harmonic convergence of what I know from Scripture (my mind), what I have surrendered to God (my will), and how my feelings influence my life (my emotions). However, we need to be careful not to just try to "pour" the Holy Spirit into our intellect, emotions or will. In the same way that mere knowledge of the Holy Spirit will not bring His filling, an abundance of emotional tears and incessant begging will also not lead to the filling of the Holy Spirit.

The more we think about the Holy Spirit controlling our lives, the less He does. The more we try to "get" the Holy Spirit into a situation, the less He comes. And the more we try to stir up our feelings, the less the Holy Spirit stirs them up. We can't treat the Holy Spirit like a lightswitch that we can flip on and off.

## IT'S ALL ABOUT RELATIONSHIP

Praying in the Spirit is not a technique to be perfected, nor is it a state to be desired. It does not imply asking the Holy Spirit in to give us solutions to our problems. It does not mean inviting the Holy Spirit into our lives so that we can feel good about ourselves or even so that we can be used in His service. Rather, praying in the Spirit means having a *relationship* with God. How do we get this relationship? By remembering that the Holy Spirit dwells within us and by completely yielding ourselves to God. We trust the Holy Sprit to guide our thoughts, control our emotions and guide our choices.

When we are praying in the Spirit, we become so actively involved in what the Spirit wants done that nothing else seems to matter—and that's when we are the happiest in our life. The quality of our experience with God becomes more fulfilling than anything that is self-induced. Our mind becomes more enlightened through the power of the Spirit than it could ever become through study, research or investigation. And for those of us who have a disciplined will, we make better choices that lead us toward life's foremost goal—to know Christ and to make Him known—than we could ever achieve through our own self-effort.

Praying in the Spirit is a challenge that will lift us higher than we've ever been before. We don't break the rules—natural or spiritual—but we pray with intense concentration . . . with agonizing emotions . . . and with a resolute will. And to what end? To glorify God.

# YOUR ASSIGNMENT

*Yield to the Holy Spirit.* Try allowing the Holy Spirit to control your quiet time. Just remain still before the Lord and *wait* for Him to speak to you (you may want to review chapter 23). Remember, praying in the Spirit is something God does. You cannot intentionally make a Spirit-filled life happen or energize yourself into praying in the Spirit. It's all about being in a right relationship with God so that the Holy Spirit can fill you and use you.

*Don't think of things to pray.* Relax in the presence of the Lord and let the Holy Spirit bring to mind issues to pray about. Allow the Holy Spirit to give you a burden for a request, and then present that request before God.

*Pray boldly and in faith.* When the Holy Spirit puts a request upon your heart, that's the time to take action and to follow His lead. Receive God's power and pray boldly because you have confidence that your request is within the will and purpose of God.

*Think about how you feel when you are filled with the Holy Spirit.* I'd like to see a heart-rhythm or Holter-monitor readout of the times that I've been filled with the Spirit. When I'm discouraged or have just failed in a task, my system slows down, my thinking is dulled, and I feel as if I've just fallen into a ditch. But when I'm filled with the Spirit, my intellect and emotions are heightened and my whole life glows with a positive fire. How would you describe the way that you feel when God pours His Holy Spirit into your life?

# prayers of crucifixion

*But God forbid that I should boast except in the cross of our Lord Jesus Christ, by whom the world has been crucified to me, and I to the world.*

GALATIANS 6:14

An unusual rite of penitence takes place each year on Good Friday in the small farming towns and fishing villages in the Philippines. As tourists and journalists look on, a number of Filipino men—in an attempt to personally identify with the suffering and crucifixion of Christ—flog themselves in the streets and then are crucified on wooden crosses. One man, a 43-year-old fish store owner, has gone through this ritual 13 times in the past—and vows to go through two more.

Self-crucifixion has been one of the most abused phenomena of Christianity. Many people, perhaps misinterpreting Paul's statement in Galatians 5:24 that "those who are Christ's have crucified the flesh with its passions and desires," have whipped themselves, gashed their scalps by placing crude crowns of thorns on their heads, or even allowed themselves to be nailed to a cross on Good Friday. Others have starved themselves or isolated themselves in monastic towers, all in an attempt to "crucify" the flesh. But none of these are what God intended when He asked us to become crucified with Christ.

## DYING TO OUR OWN EFFORTS

Notice that when Paul states that he has been "crucified with Christ" (Gal. 2:20), he is not *initiating* the crucifixion but *receiving* it. "For I through the law died to the law that I might live to God" (v. 19). This is a past-tense action: Christ was crucified in the past, and Paul identifies with what has already happened. When we crucify ourselves, what we are really doing is identifying with Christ and putting our worldly desires to death in God's eyes. When we do this, we become crucified with Christ, and our earthly desires no longer appeal to us. Like Paul, we just want to put an end to sin in our lives.

The *prayer of crucifixion* is more about yielding ourselves to God than it is about aggressively dealing with sin. It is more about receiving the Christ's power than it is about seeking to crush the sinful desire in our hearts. It is more about yielding to Jesus and receiving His life in exchange for our sin than it is about our own efforts to seek redemption. Jesus told His followers to take up their cross daily and follow Him (see Luke 9:23). So when we pray the prayer of crucifixion, we take up all that the cross symbolizes—humiliation, degradation, death—and identify with the pain and trials of Christ.

Jesus said, "For whoever desires to save his life will lose it, but whoever loses his life for My sake will save it" (Luke 9:24). When we pray the prayer of crucifixion, we "lose" our lives by giving up our earthly desires in order to pursue what Jesus desires. Like Paul, we strive not to "boast" about anything in life besides the cross of Christ (Gal. 6:14). We surrender our ego and our self-image to God.

When we pray the prayer of crucifixion, we become completely yielded . . . completely abandoned . . . and completely transparent before God. We quit caring what the world thinks of us and instead focus on what Jesus thinks of us and what we think about Jesus. Crucifying ourselves with Christ does not mean that we act out a role or seek to do something noteworthy to prove our sincerity to God. It means completely surrendering ourselves to God and allowing Jesus to act within us—by allowing Christ to "play out" His role in our lives.

## DYING TO OUR EARTHLY DESIRES

It is amazing how much the opinions of others control our lives. We all want to be big shots in the eyes of friends so that we will be loved and accepted. We all play various roles throughout the day to make ourselves look good because we fear that if people see us for who we truly are, they won't want to be around us. The prayer of crucifixion brings freedom to our life. We block out the chatter of other people and no longer pay attention to what they say or worry about being good enough in their eyes. We listen to the voice of God and seek to find Jesus Christ in every part of our life. We become like John the Baptist and in complete humility say, "He must increase, but I must decrease" (John 3:30).

The prayer of crucifixion releases our inner compulsions toward possessions, power, glory or success. When we allow ourselves to be crucified, we take our selfish dreams and let them die at the cross. We no longer have to always win in life—we learn that losing to God is much more satisfying than winning in the world. For when we lose to God, we ultimately gain the most important thing in life—God's will!

I once paddled the Mississippi River near St. Louis, Missouri, with a friend in a sailing canoe. The current was very strong, and even with both of us paddling as hard as we could, we made little headway against the swift waters. But a limp piece of canvas sail made all the difference. When we hoisted the sail, the wind popped the sail and the canoe sliced through the current as it were not there. The same thing happens in our prayers of crucifixion. We die to our self-energy and find a greater energy. We die to our self-ambition and find a greater reason for living. We die to our own efforts against sin and yield to the powerful wind of the Holy Spirit that drives us forward.

## DYING TO OUR OWN SENSE OF IMPORTANCE

Think about what would happen if you were to die today. This is a sobering thought, because most of us live in the center of our world and can't imagine how life would go on without us. But life went on as usual before we were born, and it will do so after we're gone. So, let's face it—we're not necessary to life. However, when we *learn* to die, we become much more necessary to God.

My friend Clyde Parker, pastor of First Wesleyan Church in Highpoint, North Carolina, told me at a breakfast meeting back in 1985, "I believe my work in this church is coming to an end. I am looking for another place of ministry." Little did I know that the next day, Clyde would die in a plane accident. Clyde's great church, its dynamic missionary outreach, and his family all revolved around him. They were devastated and unsure of how to go on.

The morning after Clyde was killed in a plane accident, I felt compelled to phone Clyde's wife, Ernestine, and say, "The sun came up this morning, Ernestine, and life goes on. So must you." Little did I know that almost 20 years later, I would hear the exact same message from Ernestine when my son, a 45-year-old professor at Liberty University, was killed in a car accident. Like Clyde, a great ministry revolved around him, and our family was devastated. It was difficult to imagine how life could go on without him. But the day after his funeral at around 6:00 A.M., Ernestine called me to say, "Dr. Towns, the sun came up this morning. Life goes on, and so must you."

We need to put ourselves to death and realize how insignificant we are to this life, but how important we are to God. God loves us and has a plan for our lives. When we find God's plan and do it, we put God at the center of our life. And isn't this the place where God should be?

Crucifying ourselves with Christ implies an act of *humility* on our part. "Humility" is an interesting word—it comes from the Latin word *humus,* which means "from the earth." Humus is a rich organic soil that is formed from the partial decomposition of plant or animal matter. Think about this for a moment—the rich soil that is needed for life and growth comes from the death of other matter. When we humble ourselves in the sight of God through the prayer of crucifixion, our hearts become a rich soil for spiritual growth (see Jas. 4:10).

## PLANTING THE SEED

So how do we pray a prayer of crucifixion? Again, look at the word "humility." Humility is the act of being humble. *Webster Dictionary's* states that the word "humble" means "to reduce one-self to the lowest position in one's own eyes or in the eyes of another."[1] Humility (*humus*) is to our life what prayer is to our relationship with God. When we keep our face close to the earth, we stop thinking more highly of ourselves than we ought to think (see Rom. 12:3). We begin giving life to other people.

Does our life represent a *seed* that can be planted so that it will grow and bring forth fruit for other people? Is our life open to receiving the rain (energy) from God? In the parable of the sower, Jesus said, "But he who received seed on the good ground is he who hears the word and understands it, who indeed bears fruit and produces: some a hundredfold, some sixty, some thirty" (Matt. 13:23). The richness of the soil, the abundance of rain, and the energy of the sun will distinguish the types of fruit that the seed in our life will produce. But that life can only be brought forth with *humus,* or humility.

Trying to receive humility is kind of like trying to force ourselves to go to sleep—it just doesn't happen when we focus on it. The more we arrogantly demand to receive humility from God, the less likely we are to receive it and the less spiritual we will become. However, even though we demand humility, there are certain things that we can do to make the probability of receiving humility from God more likely. Confessing our sins to another person is one way to bring humility into our lives. Performing acts of service to another person—especially people we don't particularly like—is another method of receiving humility.

My friend Steve Sjogren, former pastor of the Vineyard Community Church in Cincinnati, Ohio, demonstrates God's love in what he calls *servant evangelism*. He believes that small things done with great love will change the world, and he puts this belief into practice in his everyday life.

Whereas some churches organize their people to go out two by two to share the gospel and witness house to house, Steve organized his people to go out and do simple tasks to demonstrate God's love to the community. Whether it was cleaning a house for a single mom, cutting the grass for the elderly, or any other task, Steve taught his congregation to demonstrate God in the small things.

On certain occasions, Pastor Sjogren and his team would even go up to a gas station attendant and ask, "Could we clean your toilets as a practical way of showing you God's love?" If you've ever had to clean a commode—and I'm sure you have—it's a very unpleasant task. Imagine willingly offering to clean the rest room of a gas station. That's a real act of love.

Many people didn't understand what Steve was doing or what purposes he hoped to accomplish. But Steve found that servant evangelism opened the doors of people's hearts so that he could plant the seed of Christ's amazing love. People who would never sit and listen to a message about the gospel would open their hearts to Steve through the practical acts of servant-hood that his congregation performed.[2]

If you don't think cleaning toilets will humble you, try it. Cleaning bathrooms puts nails into the cross of self-crucifixion.

## AWAY FROM THE LIMELIGHT

In the end, crucifying ourselves with Christ won't happen in a "big" way. Most likely, there won't be a team of tourists or jour-nalists documenting our acts of humility and self-crucifixion—it just doesn't get the same buzz that the extravagant (and misguid-ed) acts, such as physically nailing oneself to a cross, receive.

Sure, sometimes there will be important acts of self-crucifixion, such as when a Christian student breaks up with her boyfriend because he does not know the Lord, or when a believer turns down an outstanding job opportunity because it would com-promise his walk with God, or when a Christian woman gives the money she had been saving to buy a new car to her church because she sensed a need.

But more likely, the prayer of crucifixion will occur in small-er ways as we intentionally give up our life bit by bit to God each day. These small and unrecognizable victories over self-pleasure and self-advancement will not often be seen by others, but they will lead to the greatest amount of spiritual growth in our lives.

# YOUR ASSIGNMENT

*Ask God to open your spiritual eyes.* The topic of self-crucifixion may represent a new topic for you. Your first step will be to ask God to open your spiritual eyes so that you can understand the biblical nature of self-crucifixion. Specifically, you should ask for God to show you: (1) What self-crucifixion is; (2) What it accomplishes; and (3) How it is realized.

*Study verses on self-crucifixion.* Use your concordance to look up verses containing the following words: "crucify," "crucifixion," "cross." When you read these verses, note what actions occurred in the past and what actions are required in the present. Also note what actions are positional, meaning which actions happen in the heavenlies as compared to the actions that occur in this present life.

*Yield areas of your life to God.* Begin making a list of the areas in your life that you need to submit (or "crucify") to God. Once you've listed each area, actively submit each to God. This is often easier said than done. You will most likely have an ongoing struggle with yielding some areas of your life to God.

*Begin a continuous struggle of intercession.* Try to commit those areas that seem to have an especially firm hold over your life to God in prayer each day. Sometimes these areas can't be crucified to Christ in one act of surrender.

**Notes**

1. *Webster's Dictionary,* 11th edition, s.v. "humble."
2. Steve Sjogren, *Community of Kindness* (Ventura, CA: Regal Books, 2003), n.p.

# The Transforming power of prayer

*And we know that all things work together for good to those who love*
*God, to those who are the called according to [His] purpose . . .*
*[to be] transformed to the image of His Son.*

ROMANS 8:28-29, *ELT*

So, what is the purpose of prayer? In this book, we've looked at a number of different aspects concerning prayer and how we should approach the throne of God with our petitions and praise. But fundamentally, the purpose of prayer—regardless of the various forms it takes and situations in which it arises—is for us to establish and maintain a relationship with God. For when our relationship with God deepens and becomes a part of our everyday life, we begin to be transformed by God and become more like His Son, Jesus Christ. Life-changing prayer lies at the foundation of our prayer relationship with God.

In Romans 8:28, Paul states that all things work together for good to those who know God and are called according to His purpose. What is God's purpose for our life? "That we might be transformed to the image of His Son" (Rom. 8:29, *ELT*). Of course, most of us would say that we are nothing like Jesus! So the question becomes not how far short we have fallen, but what is the next thing in our life that needs to be brought into conformity with Jesus. The answer to this question is found in our prayer life. As we enter into a prayer relationship with God, He shows us where we fall short and tells us what we must do to correct that deficit.

## BE READY FOR CHANGE

When we establish a daily prayer time and seek to enter into a relationship with the Lord, we need to be ready and willing for God to change our lives. We need to open our hearts to God's transforming power and actively seek to follow His will. We need to consciously take the focus off of ourselves and strive to follow the example of Christ as laid out in Scripture. We need to remember that the purpose of prayer is not primarily to have our needs met or our circumstances changed, but that prayer functions for the greater purpose of transforming our life into the likeness of Christ.

Often, people aren't transformed through prayer because they make prayer a program. They write out a prayer list and then systematically pray for each one of those requests, but they don't allow the prayer to *change* them—it's just a routine they follow. Others spend all their prayer time asking for things, and when God answers their requests, their purposes are satisfied—they do not allow the experience to profoundly change their lives. Some pray for victory, and when they conquer something, their ego is reinforced—their prayers have changed their outer circumstances but not their inner lives. For our relationship with God to develop and mature, we need to seek the transforming power of God.

When we experience the reality of God, our life *will* change, for we cannot come face-to-face with God without being transformed in some way. When we look into the holiness of God, we realize how much sin there is in our life and we want to change. When we are enveloped in the Father's arms of love and recognize our selfishness, the discomfort we feel will compel us to want to alter our life.

Of course, this will require humility and submission to the perfect will of God for this transformation to occur. Have you ever struggled against the will of God? If you say you haven't, you are not being honest with yourself. The Word of God teaches us to be humble, but we are driven by ego. The Word of God teaches us to be holy, but we are constantly tempted by our old nature. The Word of God teaches us to put Jesus first, but our selfish nature always cries out, "Me first!" But when we honestly communicate with God, we also honestly face our own selfish nature. This view of our ego-driven life should disquiet us so much that we'll either change or quit praying.

If we don't allow prayer to change us, we become severely limited in what our future prayers can accomplish. *Prayer must change us before it can change our circumstances.* This is not to say that we can't receive answers to our prayers, but just that self-motivated prayers severely limit the abundance of God. When we refuse to change, He cannot change us into the people that He wants us to be. God can and will still work in our lives, but if we don't submit to God and allow that power to transform us, our relationship with our heavenly Father will not develop.

## THE POWER OF GOD'S LOVE

So how do we allow God to transform our life? Well, as we come into the presence of God, our first attitude must be one of submission to God and all that He wants us to do. We need to realize that just as a mechanic uses tools to repair an automobile, God uses prayer to repair our lives. Sometimes this transformation can be immediate and dramatic, but more likely God will use prayer to gradually grow us into the image of Christ.

We need to treat prayer as a personal discipline that will transform us into a dedicated disciple of Jesus Christ. When we pray well, we will follow Jesus well. So, if we do not pray (or seldom pray), we will find it difficult to follow Christ in our daily life. This is why it is critical to learn the *discipline of prayer*. If we have not learned the discipline of prayer, we probably have not learned to think, act or feel like Jesus.

We also need to allow the *love of God* to come into our lives and transform us and then share that love with those around us. Jesus stated the greatest command is to "love the Lord your God with all your heart, all your soul, and all your mind" (Matt. 22:37, *NLT*). To this, Jesus added another commandment as to how much we should love others: "You shall love your neighbor as yourself" (v. 39).

Prayer begins with us focusing on God, which draws us toward God's transformational presence. As we enter into God's presence, we reach out to Him in worship and receive His love into our life. But it doesn't stop there! The more we experience God's transformational love, the more loving we become and the more we will want to share that love with others.

Transformational prayer is all about love. Consider the example of the apostle Peter. After the crucifixion of Jesus, Peter had gone back to his fishing nets. Like most people, Peter and the disciples' primary focus had been on their jobs. Peter just couldn't get the *nets* out of his system—they were his occupational tools. When Jesus appeared to His disciples on the shore of the Sea of Galilee, He told them to cast their nets on the right side of the boat, and they would get fish.

After supernaturally providing the disciples' breakfast in this manner, Jesus approached Peter and said, "Simon, son of Jonah, do you love Me more than *these*?" (John 21:15, emphasis added). In the Greek, the context of this phrase suggests that Jesus was asking Peter if he loved Him more than the nets. Furthermore, Jesus used the Greek word *agape* to ask if Peter had self-sacrificing love for Him. All that Peter could answer was, "Yes, Lord; You know that I love You" (v. 15) using the Greek word *philo* for love, which would be similar to saying, "Yes, I like you."

That morning, Jesus asked Peter three times if he deeply loved Him—twice by using the word *agape* and the final time by using the word *philo*. Perhaps this was because Peter had denied the Lord three times after Jesus had been arrested (see John 18:15-27). When Jesus asked Peter the third time, the backslidden fisherman responded, "Lord, You know all things; You know that I love You" (John 21:17).

Do you see the conversation going back and forth between Peter and Jesus? Isn't their conversation the same as prayer—us talking with God? And what was the purpose of the conversation? Was it not to *transform* Peter from a discouraged, backslidden fisherman into a dedicated disciple? Wasn't that a *transformational prayer*?

## LET GO OF THE NETS!

Let's not get hung up on the nets in our life. The real question is *love*. Jesus is asking each of us, "Do you love *Me*?" And we need to remember that loving God without loving our neighbors is no love at all. Loving God necessarily demands that we love the people with whom we come into contact each day. Love to God can never stand alone without love to our neighbors.

So, when we look into the face of God, do we see our lost neighbors . . . our needy neighbors . . . our waiting neighbors? When we look into the face of our neighbors, can we see the presence of God calling us to come help them? Just as transformational prayer draws us upward to be like God's Son, it also draws us outward toward other people. We cannot withdraw into our shell and be an obedient follower of Christ. Transformational prayer brings us out of our shells in both upward intimacy with God and horizontal intimacy with others.

# YOUR ASSIGNMENT

*Ask God to transform your life in your daily prayer requests.* One of the best ways to receive God's transforming power in your life is to be open to it and request it from God. Just praying to be transformed will not make it happen, but it will probably never happen unless you begin asking to be transformed.

*Study biblical examples of people who were transformed.* Look up the word "transformed" in a concordance and then study some of the situations in the Bible in which people were transformed. Ask yourself the following questions: (1) Who was transformed? (2) When did this transformation occur? (3) Why did it happen? and, most importantly, (4) What happened when the person was transformed?

*Tell God that you love Him.* Think of all the reasons that you *already* love God and then tell Him those reasons in prayer. Next, think of all the other reasons why you *should* love God (reasons that are not operative in your life). The more you love God and receive His love, the more your life will be transformed.

*Write out a profile of the type of person you'd like to become.* If you think you don't have any changes to make in your life, you've missed what this book is about. Write out what attitudes you'd like to assume, what strengths you'd like to develop, and what spiritual gifts you'd like to use. Your profile may be the beginning of the journey toward spiritual transformation!

# Glossary

## THE DIFFERENT TYPES OF PRAYER

*Prayers of faith that raise up the sick and restore them to health.*

*Prayers in which we eagerly seek to enjoy God's presence.*

*Meditating in God's presence without making audible requests
or even carrying on a conversation (also known as* Praying
Without Words*).*

*Praying about even the little details of life.*

*When we pray for things in order to bring glory to ourselves
instead of sincerely speaking to God from our hearts.*

*The prayers of our troubled spirits, in which we choose to deal
with the unrepented transgressions of others (including the sins
of past generations) and accept the consequences for those sins.*

*When we use prayer as a weapon to purposefully intercede against
the evil we encounter in this world and right the wrongs therein.*

*Prayers in which we enjoy intimate fellowship with God.*

*Prayers in which we search for the sin in our life.*

**Lord's Prayer** . . . . . . . . . . . . . . . . . . . . . . . . . . . . . . . . . . 2, 7, 24
*A model prayer that was given to us by Jesus in Matthew 6:9-13 and Luke 11:2-4. The Lord's Prayer contains all of the elements that are necessary for effective prayer.*

**Praise, Prayers of** . . . . . . . . . . . . . . . . . . . . . . . . . . . . . . . . . . . 6
*When we focus on God in prayer to compliment Him for who He is and what He has done in our lives.*

**Prayer Excursions** . . . . . . . . . . . . . . . . . . . . . . . . . . . . . . . . . . . 7
*When a group of people journey to a specific location that is in need of prayer.*

**Prayer Journeys** . . . . . . . . . . . . . . . . . . . . . . . . . . . . . . . . . . . . . 7
*When people walk from one destination to another while praying for the specific needs of those along their routes.*

**Prayer Walking** . . . . . . . . . . . . . . . . . . . . . . . . . . . . . . . . . . . . . 7
*When individuals or groups of people come together to walk around their neighborhoods to pray for the people who live there: "Praying on sight with insight."*

**Praying in Jesus' Name** . . . . . . . . . . . . . . . . . . . . . . . . . . . . . . 4
*An act by which we can enter into a relationship with Jesus Christ, take full advantage of His death on the cross as payment for our sins, and accept Him as the Lord over our life.*

**Praying in the Spirit** . . . . . . . . . . . . . . . . . . . . . . . . . . . . . . . . 25
*Allowing the Holy Spirit to make requests through our prayers to God the Father.*

**Prevailing Prayers** . . . . . . . . . . . . . . . . . . . . . . . . . . . . . . . . . . 13
*Continually interceding in prayer until we receive an answer from God.*

For more information about prayer, please visit:

**www.elmertowns.com**